Marc Wolter

Navigation in Time-Varying Scientific Data

Marc Wolter

Navigation in Time-Varying Scientific Data

Intuitive and interactive navigation
through time-varying simulation data

Südwestdeutscher Verlag für Hochschulschriften

Impressum/Imprint (nur für Deutschland/ only for Germany)
Bibliografische Information der Deutschen Nationalbibliothek: Die Deutsche Nationalbibliothek verzeichnet diese Publikation in der Deutschen Nationalbibliografie; detaillierte bibliografische Daten sind im Internet über http://dnb.d-nb.de abrufbar.

Alle in diesem Buch genannten Marken und Produktnamen unterliegen warenzeichen-, markenoder patentrechtlichem Schutz bzw. sind Warenzeichen oder eingetragene Warenzeichen der jeweiligen Inhaber. Die Wiedergabe von Marken, Produktnamen, Gebrauchsnamen, Handelsnamen, Warenbezeichnungen u.s.w. in diesem Werk berechtigt auch ohne besondere Kennzeichnung nicht zu der Annahme, dass solche Namen im Sinne der Warenzeichen- und Markenschutzgesetzgebung als frei zu betrachten wären und daher von jedermann benutzt werden dürften.

Verlag: Südwestdeutscher Verlag für Hochschulschriften Aktiengesellschaft & Co. KG
Dudweiler Landstr. 99, 66123 Saarbrücken, Deutschland
Telefon +49 681 37 20 271-1, Telefax +49 681 37 20 271-0
Email: info@svh-verlag.de
Zugl.: Aachen, RWTH, Diss., 2010

Herstellung in Deutschland:
Schaltungsdienst Lange o.H.G., Berlin
Books on Demand GmbH, Norderstedt
Reha GmbH, Saarbrücken
Amazon Distribution GmbH, Leipzig
ISBN: 978-3-8381-1923-6

Imprint (only for USA, GB)
Bibliographic information published by the Deutsche Nationalbibliothek: The Deutsche Nationalbibliothek lists this publication in the Deutsche Nationalbibliografie; detailed bibliographic data are available in the Internet at http://dnb.d-nb.de.

Any brand names and product names mentioned in this book are subject to trademark, brand or patent protection and are trademarks or registered trademarks of their respective holders. The use of brand names, product names, common names, trade names, product descriptions etc. even without a particular marking in this works is in no way to be construed to mean that such names may be regarded as unrestricted in respect of trademark and brand protection legislation and could thus be used by anyone.

Publisher: Südwestdeutscher Verlag für Hochschulschriften Aktiengesellschaft & Co. KG
Dudweiler Landstr. 99, 66123 Saarbrücken, Germany
Phone +49 681 37 20 271-1, Fax +49 681 37 20 271-0
Email: info@svh-verlag.de

Printed in the U.S.A.
Printed in the U.K. by (see last page)
ISBN: 978-3-8381-1923-6

Copyright © 2010 by the author and Südwestdeutscher Verlag für Hochschulschriften Aktiengesellschaft & Co. KG and licensors
All rights reserved. Saarbrücken 2010

ACKNOWLEDGEMENTS

This thesis has been written during my work at the Virtual Reality Group at RWTH Aachen University. I would not have accomplished the task of writing this thesis without the direct or indirect support of many people over the last years. First of all, I would like to thank my advisor Prof. Torsten Kuhlen for his support in the making of this thesis and the necessary scientific environment to let ideas grow. I am also grateful to Prof. Oliver Staadt for acting as a co-referee for this thesis. Sincere thanks go to Prof. Christian Bischof for his support throughout the years.

Discussing ideas is an essential part of research. Several people gave me useful input for my ideas, and I would like to name the most important ones here, who spent hours of their life discussing my ideas: Irene Tedjo-Palczynski, who was a great help with the user studies, Marc Schirski, who always found a counterexample for a bad idea, and Ingo Assenmacher, who always tried to keep me sound in mind. Last but not least, Bernd Hentschel, who gave merciless feedback and whose vast knowledge of literature was extremely helpful. Kind thanks go to Christian Vogt for proof-reading my thesis from a physicists point of view, Daniel Bündgens for keeping the stuff running, and all my other colleagues who gave me valuable support.

Finally, I thank my friends and family, in particular my brother Frank who awaked my interest in computers and provided me with hardware all the time, as well as my parents, who gave me the opportunity to conduct my studies in computer science. I am infinitely grateful to my wife Alexandra, for her support, patience, and just for being there.

CONTENTS

1. Introduction   **1**
     1.1. Motivation 1
     1.2. Contributions 3
     1.3. Outline 4

2. Related Work   **7**
     2.1. Time-Varying Visualization Techniques 7
     2.2. Time Models 10
     2.3. User Interfaces for Time-Varying Data 11
     2.4. Temporal Subsampling 15
     2.5. Parallel Systems for Time-Varying Visualization 17

3. A Time Model for Time-Varying Scientific Data   **21**
     3.1. Introduction 21
     3.2. Requirements 22
     3.3. Time model 23
     3.4. Time operations 27
     3.5. Application 31
     3.6. Summary and Discussion 36

4. User Interfaces for Time Navigation   **37**
     4.1. Introduction 37
     4.2. Task Analysis 38
     4.3. 3D User Interfaces 42
     4.4. Summary and Discussion 50

5. Target Selection using 3D Direct Manipulation — 53
  5.1. Introduction 53
  5.2. Basic Concepts 54
  5.3. Technique: Direct Dragging Along Trajectories 57
  5.4. Technique: Time Buoy 61
  5.5. Technique: Region Query 63
  5.6. Evaluation 66
  5.7. Summary and Discussion 71

6. Importance-Based Temporal Subsampling — 73
  6.1. Introduction 73
  6.2. Temporal Importance 75
  6.3. Importance Functions 76
  6.4. Subsampling Algorithm 81
  6.5. Results 89
  6.6. Summary 101

7. A Parallel System for Time-Varying Visualizations — 103
  7.1. Introduction 103
  7.2. Viracocha Architecture 104
  7.3. Improving Computation of Time-Varying Visualizations 106
  7.4. Scheduling Strategies 110
  7.5. Results 121
  7.6. Summary and Discussion 131

8. Summary and Conclusion — 133

A. Terminology — 137
  A.1. Overview of the Time Model 137
  A.2. Terms and Definitions 138

B. Implementation Details — 141
  B.1. Time Model 141
  B.2. Improving Performance 142

C. Data Sets — 145
  C.1. Nasal Airflow 145
  C.2. Geothermal Reservoir Simulation 146
  C.3. Ventricular Assist Device 147
  C.4. Metal Forming Process Chain 148

References — 161

CHAPTER 1

INTRODUCTION

1.1. Motivation

With the growing size, availability and performance of parallel computer systems, researchers numerically simulate increasingly complex phenomena. In order to gain insight into the simulated processes, a human researcher has to analyze the large amount of data that is generated by numerical simulations. Scientific visualization is an essential tool in this data analysis process. As a special field of general data visualization, it is primarily concerned with visualization of 3D phenomena that may change over time (which is in the following called 4D data). Scientific visualization is often preferable to other analysis techniques (e.g., statistical analysis) because it exploits the human visual pattern–recognition skills and therefore strongly contributes to the understanding of complex or unanticipated correlations. The usage of Virtual Reality (VR) technology further exploits human perception by incorporating user-centered stereoscopic projection, multimodal interfaces and direct interaction. For the interactive analysis of highly complex phenomena, this combination of scientific visualization and VR is gaining more and more importance (e.g., [69, 80]).

While the spatial resolution of simulation data is increasing, the most complex phenomena are inherently time-varying. This results at the same time in an increase of the temporal resolution. Simulations described by thousands of discrete time steps are getting common these days; simulations with a much higher resolution exist.

In this thesis, I will use the term *large time-varying data* for such data sets with a large number of

1

CHAPTER 1. INTRODUCTION

discrete time steps (i.e., thousand and multiples thereof), independent of the spatial size of a single time step, which is distinct from the same term often used for tera- or peta-scale computing. When analyzing simulation data with such a high temporal resolution, two basic problems emerge:

(1) *The Interaction Problem*: With the growing temporal resolution of simulation data, the requirement for more efficient and accurate interaction techniques that are used to organize or to maneuver through time-varying data arises. To efficiently navigate through a large amount of discrete time steps, a simulation expert needs a user interface that supports all tasks emerging in the analysis process—e.g., finding a specific time step, focusing on a time interval or choosing a suitable temporal subsampling—in an intuitive and accurate way.

(2) *The Computation Problem*: The standard approach to visualize time-varying data still is to apply known time-independent visualization techniques to all time steps in order to generate an animation. For large time-varying data this produces an enormous computational load due to the sheer amount of discrete time steps. Even for fast visualization of a single time step, the multiplication of computation time by several orders of magnitude impedes interactive visualization. Particulary for a VR-based data analysis, maintaining an interactive work flow is of major importance.

To the best of my knowledge, existing visualization systems are oblivious to both problems. The interaction techniques provided by free or commercial visualization software are meant to navigate in 10–100 time steps, but are insufficient for large time-varying data. Computational support for time-varying data is mostly given by efficient algorithms for single time step data, which is still insufficient for large numbers of discrete time steps, even for moderate single time step sizes.

This thesis proposes and evaluates techniques that tackle these two problems for large time-varying data. Its goal is to support scientists in their data analysis when investigating simulation data with a large amount of time steps. Because the topic of large time-varying data—in particular the *interaction problem*—has not been intensively addressed by the visualization community in the past, this thesis tries to introduce a conceptual foundation for this field of research. This includes the definition of formalisms to describe time as well as efficient data structures to represent time-varying data. In addition, common tasks that users execute to navigate through time are analyzed and organized in a taxonomy.

These two basic principles—a model to describe time and interaction with time as well as a classification of temporal navigation tasks—enable the development and evaluation of new interaction techniques as well as algorithms that support the identified user tasks. This thesis proposes three such new approaches. In order to address the *interaction problem*, a new 3D user interface to navigate through time has been developed. To resolve the *computation problem*, two different approaches are introduced. On the one hand, reducing the shown temporal resolution in a meaningful way reduces the necessary computational load. On the other hand, exploiting parallel computing resources with user-centered scheduling strategies reduces the overall computation time even for a large number of discrete time steps. Both approaches can be combined to interactively deal with large time-varying data.

This thesis does not propose new visualization techniques, but supportive techniques and algorithms that can be integrated in scientific visualization tools and that can be used in combination with a large number of visualization techniques. The techniques proposed in this thesis enable the analysis of large time-varying data in an interactive work process. Such an interactive exploration process will provide a major benefit for scientists who today are restricted to a cumbersome investigation of a small number of single discrete time steps.

1.2. Contributions

The contribution of this thesis is a comprehensive set of methods that render an interactive exploration of large time-varying data possible. In summary, the main contributions of this thesis are:

- A time model as a formalism to describe temporal characteristics and relations in scientific visualizations in an efficient and consistent way.

- A taxonomy for the user's temporal navigation task in the scientific data analysis process.

- Novel 3D interaction techniques that are based on direct manipulation for the task of temporal navigation.

- A stochastical optimization algorithm that computes a temporal subsampling—by selecting a subset of the available time steps—for a given set of criteria.

- A scalable parallel software system for computation of time-varying visualization data, including scheduling strategies that incorporate the user's temporal navigation interaction.

1.2.1. Publications

Parts of the research results of this thesis have been discussed in a number of publications. The time model for scientific visualization was described in [104]. Applications using this time model were presented in [52] and [105]. The direct manipulation techniques were discussed in [109, 111]. The parallel computation system was applied to time-varying data in several projects [53, 54, 110]. User-centered scheduling strategies were introduced in [106, 108].

1.3. Outline

This thesis is structured as follows: Chapter 2 gives an overview of related work from the fields of scientific visualization, human-computer interaction and parallel computing. Where appropriate, work from different fields of research is discussed. This chapter is meant to give an overview only, detailed comparisons and differences are discussed in the respective chapters.

In Chapter 3, a time model that captures the different temporal characteristics occuring in scientific visualizations is proposed. The goal of this chapter is to provide a terminology to describe both interaction and computation techniques as well as to introduce an efficient data structure on which these techniques are going to build.

Chapter 4 describes an analysis of common temporal navigation tasks that results in a taxonomy of these tasks. Based on this taxonomy, possible 3D user interfaces for scientific visualization inside virtual environments are discussed. In the following two chapters, two identified user tasks are then analyzed in more detail: movement tasks in the temporal domain as well as the task of modifying the shown temporal resolution.

For efficient execution of movement tasks, a new user interface that follows a 3D direct manipulation interaction style is proposed and evaluated in Chapter 5. This new interface addresses the *interaction problem* of large time-varying data by exploiting the intuitive interaction capabilities provided by VR.

In order to adapt the discrete temporal resolution to the user's analysis, Chapter 6 proposes a new approach to specify and compute a non-uniform resolution based on different notions of importance. Besides introducing user interfaces to specify temporal resolution, this approach mainly addresses the *computational problem* by means of reduction of the temporal resolution of large time-varying data.

To further alleviate the *computational problem*, Chapter 7 describes a distributed system that uses hybrid parallelization to handle computations on large time-varying data within acceptable waiting times—as demanded by VR-based exploration. By exploiting resources provided by parallel machines, this system provides a scalable solution for the growing size of large time-varying data. Based on this parallel system, computation strategies that incorporate the user's interaction are introduced. These strategies rely on the previously proposed task taxonomy and try to exploit assumptions about the user's interaction behavior to optimize computations.

Results for the proposed techniques will be shown directly after the techniques' description. The presented use cases and evaluations utilize simulation data sets from different fields of research (i.e., medicine, engineering, geophysics). Finally, Chapter 8 summarizes the thesis and draws conclusions from the achieved results.

The described techniques are realized in the ViSTA FlowLib visualization software [87]. The technical embedding into this Virtual Reality framework allows a straightforward use of the developed methods within multiple virtual environments. Most technical details concerning the used VR hardware are encapsulated by ViSTA FlowLib and are therefore left out in this thesis.

A list of used terms and definitions that are used throughout this thesis is listed in Appendix A. Technical details that are not necessary to understand the techniques proposed in this thesis, but which are useful for a technical realization of these techniques, are given in Appendix B. Appendix C gives a detailed description of the data sets used in this thesis.

In the following text, I will use the first person plural (we) instead of the first person singular as in this introduction, because the described work was partially elaborated in close cooperation with my co-workers, which includes useful discussions, provision of source code and numerous other support.

CHAPTER 2

RELATED WORK

This chapter discusses selected work from the fields of scientific visualization and Virtual Reality, in addition to work related to time-varying data from other fields of research. As each original work possibly discusses multiple aspects of time-varying data at once, the same work can occur multiple times in different sections. Though, it will only be discussed with respect to the appropriate topic of this section.

2.1. Time-Varying Visualization Techniques

To analyze different aspects of time-varying scientific data, various scientific visualization algorithms exist. In this section, a classification for time-varying visualization techniques is introduced and a selection of techniques is discussed exemplarily.

In the context of this thesis, we propose to distinguish two categories: visualization algorithms that process discrete time steps independently from each other (*time-independent visualization techniques*) and algorithms that process time steps in a way that introduces a dependency between single time steps (*time-dependent visualization techniques*). This classification is crucial to identify visualization algorithms that can benefit from the techniques proposed in Chapters 6 and 7, because these techniques change the order of time steps. Therefore, only *time-independent* visualization algorithms are compatible with the techniques introduced in Chapters 6 and 7.

CHAPTER 2. RELATED WORK

2.1.1. Time-Dependent Visualization Algorithms

Time-dependent visualization algorithms are algorithms that require multiple time steps in order to work and introduce a dependency between single time steps. Two prominent examples for time-dependent visualization algorithms are particle tracing and tracking the evolution of identified features. Both techniques require at least two time steps simultaneously and therefore enforce a dependency between single time steps: in particle tracing at least two time steps are necessary to interpolate the particle velocity between discrete time steps, in feature tracking two candidate features in successive time steps have to be matched.

Particle tracing visualizations try to illustrate time-varying flow structures directly. It bases on the idea of depicting the movement of matter through the simulated flow (see Weiskopf and Erlebacher for an overview [103]). Work on particle tracing deals with the computational effort of interactive particle tracing (e.g., by precomputation [15, 35, 94] or data reduction [86]), intuitive and efficient depiction of large amounts of particles (e.g., by tubelet depiction that show the evolution of a path [88]), and seeding techniques for particle tracing (e.g., by defining spatial importance functions to decide spatial density of seed points [19]).

The basic idea behind feature detection and tracking is to automatically extract physically meaningful time-varying patterns from the raw data and thereby to reduce the amount of information the user needs to analyze (see Post et al. for an overview of feature detection and tracking techniques [79]). For time-dependent data sets, one problem is detecting the correspondence between features in successive time steps that actually represent the same feature at different times. Post et al. report three approaches to solve this correspondence problem: direct extraction from the spatio-temporal domain, region-based, and attribute-based correspondence for extracted features in separate time steps [79]. Along the tracked evolution of a feature, interesting phenomena of the evolution can be detected, which are called events [82]. Possible events are, for instance, birth and death of a feature or interactions between multiple features. This extracted and reduced information is presented to the user for further investigation of the underlying simulation data.

Beside these two common visualization techniques, specialized time-dependent visualization techniques were proposed for special problems. For instance, Jänicke et al. [60] use mutual information to define local statistical complexity as the minimal amount of information required to determine the causal state of a spatio-temporal point from its past. To this end, not only the temporal past of a point x, but its past "light cone"—all points that may influence x given an assumed finite speed—are evaluated. Their approach automatically extracts rare spatial patterns in the time-varying data. As a second example, Woodring and Shen introduced a wavelet-based technique to automatically discover trends at different temporal resolutions [112]. Using wavelets, they cluster time curves of single data points into curves with similar time activity within the same scale.

2.1. TIME-VARYING VISUALIZATION TECHNIQUES

To analyze all decomposed curves resulting from a data set, clusters of curves with similar time activity (within similar scales) are formed.

This is only a selection from the large number of time-dependent visualization algorithms. Time-dependent algorithms that extract some sort of motion like particle traces or feature tracking are a prerequisite for the direct manipulation interaction techniques proposed in Chapter 4. As already mentioned, the sampling and scheduling algorithms introduced in Chapters 6 and 7 are not applicable to these time-dependent algorithms, as they change the computational order of discrete time steps. These algorithms can only be used in combination with time-independent visualization algorithms.

2.1.2. Time-Independent Visualization Algorithms

Time-independent visualization algorithms are algorithms that process multiple time steps independently from each other. These algorithms can be applied to discrete time steps of a time-varying data set in order to generate a discrete sequence of visualization objects. This sequence is mostly displayed in an animation, as this corresponds to the natural perception of time. This is the approach of most visualization systems supporting time-varying data (e.g., ParaView, Visit, EnSight). In addition, such an animation is also capable of conveying time-dependent visualization algorithms.

The class of time-independent algorithms includes algorithms operating on scalar data (e.g., contours or direct volume rendering), vector data (e.g., hedgehogs or glyphs), tensor data (e.g., tensor ellipsoids) or geometry (e.g., resampling or cutting). Details on these time-independent visualization algorithms can be found in the Visualization Handbook [49].

In order to apply time-independent visualization techniques to large time-varying simulation data sets, these algorithms or systems need to be able to cope with the enormous amount of data. Reducing the amount of data to process by discarding whole time steps (temporal sampling) is considered in Section 2.4. Systems that use parallelism to process large time-varying data are discussed in Section 2.5.

Another possible solution is to integrate spatio-temporal data structures that speed up access to time-varying data by exploiting temporal coherency. The fundamental idea of these data structures is that, even though proceeding in time is related to changing data, data changes only slightly or only locally. The Temporal Hierarchical Index Tree is used to speed up isosurface extraction from time-varying data [91]. For a grid that does not change over time, cells in a time-varying field are classified according to the temporal variation of their extreme values and are stored in a binary tree structure. Differential Time-Histogram Tables (DTHT) introduced by Younesy et al. [113] store 2D (time and isovalue bins) histograms. In each bin, the active set and the differentials to adjacent bins are stored. Differential cells are stored both in the temporal and isovalue direction of the histogram. Using a DTHT, gradual changes in the query values (both isovalue and time) can be answered by discarding/adding just the differential cells. Other examples are the Time-Space Partitioning (TSP) [92] or Temporal Branch-on-Need tree (TBON) [96], which are based on an octree data structure. All these data structures provide a satisfactory reduction of the memory access during visualization computation. While the data structures themselves are time-dependent, they are generally used for time-independent algorithms. But, as each is optimized to a specific visualization technique, these data structures are not usable as optimizations for general time-independent visualization algorithms.

2.2. Time Models

To the best of our knowledge, Bryson et al. [16, 18] were the first to discuss time management in the context of Virtual Reality applications for scientific visualization. The authors distinguish six senses of time that correspond to the time stamps of single steps in the processing of time-varying data. This time model is also used to describe consistent operations on time-varying data, e.g., only the latest computed data is shown. However, their time management structure is deeply related to their software structure and therefore not applicable as a general model. Nonetheless, as they address the problem of visualizing time-varying data in a consistent way, their model of time is closely related to this thesis.

Several visualization applications that support displaying time-varying data sets exist, which therefore inherently possess some model of time. However, these time models are rarely described explicitly but must be deduced from user interfaces or application programming interfaces (APIs). The commercial EnSight software [25] provides a user interface for mixing continuous and discrete data. In addition, visualization of data objects with different temporal information, so-called time-sets, is enabled using a composite timeline. Using these timesets, several simulation objects can be integrated in a single visualization session. However, as the technical realization is embedded in a commercial system, the underlying model is not applicable to other systems. The ParaView software [67] distinguishes three time frames: an animation time that changes when animation is playing, a reader time that corresponds to time stamps associated with data files (all readers must use the same time unit), and an application time that is used to request data from VTK components (which is typically the same as animation time, but constant values or keyframes are also possible). Again, this model is strongly connected to the corresponding VTK modules and inadequate for our requirements (see Section 3.2).

In addition, different time models exist in other disciplines, which fulfill requirements different from the ones we are going to describe in Section 3.2. In the field of information visualization, Aigner et al. [4] recently introduced a taxonomy for time-dependent visualization. It is more complex than required for scientific visualization, as information visualization deals with the visualization of abstract data instead of only 3D/4D data. This data can consist of time points as well as time intervals, or time may branch into different alternatives. Aigner et al. [4] demand more effort in the research related to interaction with time-oriented data, a topic we contribute to here.

Even the model of physical time itself—i.e., the time we live in—has been topic of early philosophical discussions. For instance, Aristoteles' and Newton's models of time differ with respect to the necessity of an external reference:

Aristoteles writes

> "It is evident then that neither time is a motion nor can exist without a motion."
> - (from Aristotle's Physica, written 350 B.C., translation by Apostle [6])

In contrast, Newton states that

> "Absolute, true and mathematical time, of itself, and from its own nature, flows equably without regard to anything external, and by another name is called duration; relative, apparent, and common time is some sensible and external (whether accurate or unequable) measure of duration by the means of motion, which is commonly used instead of true time; such as an hour, a day, a month, a year."
> - (from Newton's Principia, first published in 1686, translated and edited by Cajori [20])

All these different time models try to capture the properties of time as they are necessary for specific problems. There are time models in scientific visualization, but these are strongly related to specific implementations of visualization applications, and do not consider interaction nor the requirements we identify in Section 3.2.

2.3. User Interfaces for Time-Varying Data

Before discussing user interfaces for time navigation, the users' tasks done during navigation need to be identified. Several publications provide classifications and taxonomies for common tasks in scientific data analysis, but none explicitly includes time navigation. At the first IEEE Visualization conference, Wehrend et al. proposed a list of nine general user goals (identify, locate, distinguish, categorize, cluster, rank, compare, associate, correlate), which were deduced from a review of over 300 visual displays [102]. Springmeyer divides user tasks into three general tasks: managing the data, applying math and recording ideas [95]. Casner proposes only two general user analysis tasks, search and computation [22], where computation tasks involve a transformation of the data, while search tasks do not. Another classification is possible by regarding the scope of an analysis task. Robertson distinguishes point, local, and global scope [83]—i.e., a particular location, a small subregion, and the entire data. Haimes and Darmofal use the scope to classify user analysis tasks: probing a particular location, feature identification within regions of the data, and scanning through the entire data set [48]. These task analyses are either general descriptions of the scientific data analysis process or focus on spatial characteristics of the data. Therefore, they do not address tasks concerning the temporal aspects of the simulation data, but provide a useful basis for the task taxonomy we are going to introduce in Section 4.2.

The task of browsing in a large data space, for instance in text documents, has been researched for different media. According to Hürst et al., continuous data can be interpreted as a stream of single frames [59]. Therefore, browsing in a video or animation is comparable to scrolling in a text document.

While scrollbars are the predominant interaction technique for browsing, they possess several drawbacks [116]: their usage shifts the locus of attention away from the target, and time is required to acquire the wiper element. In addition, they yield only a limited resolution (e.g., one pixel for 2D scrollbars). This results in the inability of precisely selecting desired items that are below the provided granularity.

To counteract the latter problem, Ahlberg and Shneiderman [1] proposed the Alphaslider to navigate in large lists of alphanumeric data. This technique enables the user to select between fine or coarse movement of the slider thumb. To the best of our knowledge, techniques such as the Alphaslider are not used in visualization systems. The TimeSlider technique [68] was designed to select time instants in a long time scale. The user interface employs a non-linear and moving visible time scale to allow a precise selection of specific time instants. However, evaluation showed that the performance using the TimeSlider is comparable to the performance of common slider-based position controls.

In spite of their drawbacks, the user interface techniques most commonly found for temporal navigation in scientific visualization toolkits are linear time sliders, which are combined with VCR-like buttons (i.e., play, stop, one step forwards, one step backwards). For instance, the ParaView software [67] supports interaction within discrete time steps in the form of VCR-like

2.3. USER INTERFACES FOR TIME-VARYING DATA

controls and a linear time slider. Animation speed control and selection of the visible time interval are possible with textual interfaces. Three different animation modes are provided: a sequence of a defined number of frames, an animation of a specific duration, and a sequence of all time steps. As in most other toolkits, the focus lies on a sequence of discrete time steps and images and not on the temporal correlation of the analyzed data. Additionally, no interaction is possible during animation.

The time slider interface can also be found in VR-based scientific visualization applications, mostly integrated as adapted 2D graphical user interface (GUI) integrated into the virtual environment. For instance, the Cloud Explorer [46] provides the user with VCR-buttons, a slider-based rate control, and a linear time slider. The latter can also be used to restrict the visible time range. To counteract the problems for ray-based selection of small objects, the IntenSelect [30] technique is applied for a fast acquisition of the 3D slider elements. However, this interface still possesses the two mentioned drawbacks: limited granularity and indirect control.

While the time slider is the predominant interaction technique for time navigation in scientific visualization, some work introduced alternative interaction techniques for certain time navigation tasks. For geographic information systems (GIS), Monmonier proposed two techniques to alleviate temporal navigation: temporal focusing and temporal brushing [77]. The former allows restricting the observed time interval (also called range selection), while the latter enables the user to deselect certain temporal regions (e.g., all data from winter in a cyclic seasonal time frame). Later, Harrower et al. [50] found in a study that students using temporal brushing and focusing showed an improved understanding of the relationship between climate variables.

The VR-based CAVEvis system [61] applies a clock metaphor both as a time legend and a widget to manipulate time, i.e., time is manipulated by twisting the clock dial. However, restricting the time range is only facilitated by offline configuration of files. As the clock metaphor was not evaluated, it remains open if this metaphor has any benefits over time sliders. Edsall et al. [34], who investigated the effect of different types of temporal legends, could not find an effect when comparing linear slider legends and cyclic clock-like legends.

Hentschel et al. [52] proposed to use a static view of the trajectories of time-varying particle traces. On these trajectories, sample positions are marked with icons, which represent the associated time instant. By selecting an icon using a 3D user interface, the system jumps to the appropriate time instant. To avoid occlusion of these icons, geometry elements are made invisible when activating the static view. Even though this technique allows direct selection in the visualization space to navigate in time, the user is restricted to the selected icons.

For navigation in continuous video media, linear time sliders are also common practice in most

CHAPTER 2. RELATED WORK

media players or video editing tools. Rate controls in audio and video tools (e.g., playback speed in QuickTime Player or Windows Media Player, or fast forward controls) are common practice as well. In scientific visualization tools, they are rarely used. Time navigation in audio and video media has earlier been recognized as a problem and therefore has been discussed more extensively. As results from this field possibly apply to navigation in scientific visualizations, some selected results are described here.

Lee et al. investigated three user interfaces (a scroll ring, a jog dial, and an iPod touch wheel) for audio media [70]. Their results showed that users were able to locate a certain position 90 to 100 seconds away in a continuous audio stream faster using the two available position control devices (i.e., jog dial and touch wheel) than using the rate control scroll ring. A rate control interaction technique for video media was proposed by Hürst et al. [58]. Here, the distance between mouse and slider knob determines the scrolling speed, i.e., scrolling is slower when the mouse position is close to the slider knob and vice versa. In initial user studies the authors did not find significant differences between the standard slider and their approach.

Recently, several research activities have proposed and evaluated direct manipulation techniques to browse videos. These methods have in common that a major challenge is pre-processing of the video to compute trajectories, which can then be interactively moved to browse the video. Kimber et al. [65] presented the Trailblazing system, which uses trajectories based on people segmented from the video content. In addition to control the video directly, it also allows dragging iconic representations of the identified people on a floor map.

The DRAGON system [64] uses an optical flow field technique to precompute trajectories for each pixel. Using this information, users can drag objects along their trajectories in the video directly. DRAGON uses a "closest point" approach to select a position on the trajectory with a mouse cursor. In an evaluation of the system, users performed up to 42% faster compared to using a linear time slider.

The Direct Manipulation Video Player (DiMP) proposed by Dragicevic et al. [33] also uses precomputed pixel trajectories, but provides several optimizations, for instance, a compensation of background motions for moving cameras. In their experiments, users performed up to 250% faster than using a time slider. In addition, the authors provide a methodical background to the design of video dragging tasks. They emphasize, that these kinds of techniques are very useful when video navigation is performed to solve tasks involving space. As the latter work shows promising results, the basic idea of using direct manipulation of objects to change time is followed in Chapter 4.

2.4. Temporal Subsampling

When the existing temporal resolution is too fine to permit an efficient visualization, a temporal subsampling of the data is inevitable. While spatial downsampling also reduces the necessary amount of data, for large time-varying data sets even spatially reduced data can exceed the capabilities of visualization workstations. As spatial data reduction is not the focus of this thesis, this approach is not discussed here.

A straightforward approach to temporally sample data is a uniform subsampling. For instance, the sequence mode provided by the ParaView software [67] generates a predefined sequence of frames that are evenly spaced in the visible time interval. In contrast, for a non-uniform subsampling, single data items need to be selected from the overall data set. One possible way is to use a ranking function—i.e., some data items must be ranked above others, and are therefore more *important* than others. Therefore, a key point in the selection of new samples is the definition of the term *importance*.

Wang et al. [101] define importance by shared mutual information with neighboring discrete time steps. The idea behind this is that changes in the time-varying data are of special interest. They compute mutual information for each block of a volume to obtain importance information of spatial regions. Spatial regions can be clustered together based on the similarity of their mutual information curves. By accumulating all blocks in a time step, the importance of a single time step is computed. They adapt the temporal resolution to show more important time steps using a heuristic algorithm, which—for each segment of nearly equal importance—selects the discrete time step which maximizes mutual information with respect to the last chosen time step. We later use their approach as an example importance function, therefore it is briefly summarized in Section 6.3.3. They also propose to adapt the animation speed according to importance, in order to "fast forward" over uninteresting regions, while animating highly important parts in a "slow motion" fashion. While they address the problem of selecting a suitable temporal sampling, they incorporate only a single criterion, which is to maximize joint entropy.

Multiple criteria are used by Lu and Shen to provide the scientist with a storyboard-like temporal overview [72]. To generate this overview, representative time steps are selected based on different feature criteria. By using dissimilarity matrices over all combinations of time steps, this technique allows to incorporate multiple criteria to distinguish time steps from one another. For each criterion, a dissimilarity matrix over all combinations of time steps is computed. These matrices are composed into a single dissimilarity matrix using weighted sums. The final selection of time steps—which is performed on a lower-dimensional reduction of the dissimilarity data—is done by a greedy selection algorithm picking the time steps with the highest composed suitability values. Reduction in dimensionality is done, as the author's goal is to depict keyframes with a "pseudo-distance" showing similarity. While the approach to incorporate multiple criteria is similar to ours—which is introduced in Chapter 6—, they apply a greedy selection on a reduced set of criteria only.

A linked combination of value exploration and exploration of temporal behavior was shown by Akiba and Ma [5]. Multivariate connections can be brushed using a parallel coordinates interface, which is linked to time histograms for each brushed attribute and a direct volume rendering of selected attributes and time instants. While this provides a very explorative way to find interesting points in time, the user can only manually select single time instants, which is not suitable to define a complete temporal sampling.

Another approach that directly includes domain knowledge was presented by Glatter et al. [44]. Using this system, a domain scientist specifies uncertain temporal patterns using a description language. Temporal evolutions and multivariate connections can be formulated as queries using this language, and the system returns data points that exhibit the specified pattern. While focusing on temporal patterns, this method obtains a set of spatial points where the given patterns occur. A measure for importance in the temporal domain is not directly obtained.

The problem to identify important scenes for temporal overviews or navigation was also addressed in the field of video analysis. Several publications in this field define an importance measure to select keyframes from video data. As one example, Girgensohn et al. automatically select important scenes to provide a keyframe-based overview of the complete video [43]. Video segments are assigned an importance value that depends on the rarity and duration of the segment—rare and long segments are more important than repeated or short video scenes. To select a number of these keyframes, video frames and segments are hierarchically clustered, using the difference of color histograms as a distance function. Given the hierarchy of clusters, it is straightforward to select a set of different scenes for a given number of desired keyframes. Other work from this area exists, but video analysis differs from scientific visualization in the fact that the content of videos is unmodifiable, while generating and tuning visualizations is an essential part of scientific visualization.

While there are multiple algorithms that can be used for non-uniform temporal subsampling, no general approach that incorporates the user's domain knowledge usable in a visualization system has been introduced yet.

2.5. Parallel Systems for Time-Varying Visualization

Several parallel algorithms and systems have been proposed to cope with the data required to compute time-varying visualizations. Unless otherwise stated, systems discussed here follow a client-server paradigm, where a visualization client sends requests to a server, which then computes the results on a parallel machine. We briefly describe multiple distributed or parallel systems in order to show the variety of available systems.

The FAST system manages a central shared memory component called hub, which handles requests from connected programs [9]. These programs are connected to the hub via network sockets and implement visualization (e.g., isosurfaces or particle traces) or data manipulation algorithms (e.g., file input, calculations on fields). They manipulate the data managed by the hub using Unix System V shared memory operations.

The pV3 system uses Parallel Virtual Machine (PVM) for communication [47]. This system assumes already split-up and load-balanced tasks, which are handled using a distributed memory paradigm. On the visualization systems, threads are used to separate rendering and data collection from a network. Only geometry data is transmitted from the HPC server to the visualization client. PV3 provides two viewing modes: in the asynchronous viewing mode data is shown as soon as it is computed, in the lock-step mode data is presented in a time accurate way.

Chen et al. proposed a visualization system optimized for the EarthSimulator parallel machine [23]. Their system focuses on parallel volume rendering, but supports isosurfaces, hyperstreams, LIC volumes, and particle tracing as well. For direct volume rendering, a three-level hybrid parallelization approach is used. Here, objects are distributed via the Message Passing Interface (MPI), image space is distributed using Open Multi-Processing (OpenMP), and vectorization provides an additional performance increase. This system also provides two viewing modes, asynchronous viewing and offline generation of images without an active viewer. The work of Yu et al. [114] focuses on optimizing input and output (I/O) performance. They introduce a distributed memory parallel system that is partitioned into input processors and rendering processors. Rendering is done using the parallel volume rendering approach of Ma [73]. Two strategies to use input processors are proposed: in the 1DIP strategy, each input processor reads one time step, while in the 2DIP strategy, each group of n processors reads one time step using MPI's parallel I/O. By reducing the I/O cost, I/O is more efficiently overlapped with rendering. In all these systems, scheduling of tasks is not addressed.

Scheduling and distribution schemes are a topic in parallel direct volume rendering (DVR) (e.g., load-balancing strategies for sort-last rendering were proposed by Marchesin et al. [75]). Parallel DVR is particularly useful for spatially large data sets, where the size of the image space is significantly smaller than the data's spatial resolution. In a similar way, parallel raytracing can be efficiently used to display isosurfaces in spatially large data [74]. While the literature provides several parallel volume rendering algorithms, this work focuses on the parallelization of a specific algorithm in contrast to parallelization of visualization computations on time-varying data in general. In addition, the efficient application of remote rendering or raytracing for virtual environments—which typically possess a large image space while demanding very low latency—is still an open problem.

Data-flow oriented visualization toolkits consist of modules, which are the smallest unit of execution. Independent modules are connected to describe the flow of input data in order to solve a specific visualization task. By distributing these modules, these data-flow visualization toolkits can be used to implement three types of parallelism: task parallel, pipeline parallel, or data parallel [2]. Task parallel approaches distribute suitable heterogenous subtasks to processes, pipeline approaches distribute subtasks that are organized in a sequence, and data parallel approaches execute the same instructions on different pieces of the data. Parallel data-flow applications do not follow the client-server approach, unless a module is used as a dedicated server. As an example, the pipeline-based Visualization Toolkit (VTK) can be used to implement all three types of parallelism. While task and data parallel processing are used to speed up the computation of single time steps, pipelined processing takes advantage of the known order in time-varying data sets [2]. Recently, Biddiscombe et al. [10] described the support of temporal information in VTK. Time-dependent data is supported as discrete and continuous data, with the possibility to use interpolation to transform a set of discrete time steps into a temporally quasi-continuous source of data. Special components allow caching of already requested time steps. Adaptation of different pieces of timing information is possible with a shift-and-scale operator. This functionality was integrated in the ParaView software [67], which is based on VTK. While the authors describe an implementation for time-varying data structures and algorithms in a specific toolkit, we introduce a semantic model to use such an implementation.

Parallel computing resources have early been brought in to support scientific visualization in virtual environments. The Distributed Virtual Windtunnel (DVW) uses a network library for remote procedure calls (RPCs) [17]. The parallel DVW backend dedicates one process to handling communication, one process to file I/O, and the remaining processes to compute a visualization on the current time step. This is already a hybrid parallelization, as vectorization is applied for further optimization. The resulting geometry data is transmitted to the DVW frontend, which possesses a dedicated communication process in addition to the rendering process.

The CosmicWorm system was developed to study astrophysical phenomena in virtual environments [45]. The visualization frontend can display either archived simulation data or data from a running simulation that is connected via a high-performance Hippi/FDDM network [84]. In

2.5. PARALLEL SYSTEMS FOR TIME-VARYING VISUALIZATION

contrast to most other systems, the frontend itself is used for visualization computation and rendering, while the remote backend transmits simulation data. Time steps of the simulation are processed in a pipelined way: while time step $i+1$ is simulated, time step i is visualized and the visualization for time step $i-1$ is displayed to the user. The visualization itself uses a parallel isosurface algorithm, which is executed on a shared memory machine. On the same machine, several processes manage the virtual environment, that is, rendering, acoustics, and head-tracking.

Gerndt et al. introduced the Viracocha system, which performs computational fluid dynamics (CFD) post-processing for immersive virtual environments [40]. This system is applied as parallel backend for scientific visualization using the ViSTA FlowLib [87] frontend. Viracocha uses MPI for distributed memory parallelization of visualization algorithms on time-varying data or multi-block data. Main features of Viracocha are a streaming functionality for certain algorithms and a data management system for large CFD data. The data management caches already used data and is able to predict future data requests using several strategies [107]. Later, a hybrid parallelization to compute critical points using Viracocha was presented by Gerndt et al. [42]. Here, MPI is combined with nested OpenMP loops to achieve a good load balancing. The Viracocha system as described by Gerndt et al. [40] provides the technical foundation for Chapter 7.

A large variety of parallel visualization systems exists, some are used for general scientific visualization, others were designed especially for VR-based visualization. We introduced only a choice of available systems here. The variety shows that employing parallel computation to deal with time-varying data is a common approach. Therefore, instead of introducing a new system, we are going to focus on scheduling strategies to process large time-varying data. All the systems described here share the goal of computing visualizations with high performance and are therefore optimized for high scalability. Though, in Section 7.4.2 we are going to show that while high computing performance in general supports the user's analysis, incorporating the user's interaction into the computational process can also be beneficial to answer the analysis question faster. To the best of our knowledge, none of the described systems directly incorporates the user as a target of the computation by reacting to the user's interaction or exploration behavior.

CHAPTER 3

A TIME MODEL FOR TIME-VARYING SCIENTIFIC DATA

3.1. Introduction

The visualization of simulation data can comprise objects with heterogeneous and non-trivial temporal characteristics. This includes objects with different scales, combinations of simulations into one overall process, or recurring temporal patterns. In addition, the temporal properties of each visualization object can be described from different frames of reference: for instance, a user working with a file browser describes data by the discrete files on harddisk, while a user observing an animation of the same simulation data describes data with respect to the observed time.

In order to classify and correlate the different time frames occurring in scientific visualization, this chapter proposes a time model for time-varying scientific data. We identify three major benefits of this model:

- First, a vocabulary of concepts is established. Such a formalism enables the precise description of time-aware algorithms and temporal interaction.

- Second, the time model is beneficial as a design help for software solutions for time-varying problems. By allowing non-uniform relations between data and observed animation, and by exploiting temporal recurrence, an efficient description of time-varying data is made possible. This is particularly useful for more complex use cases, where multiple simulations or visu-

CHAPTER 3. A TIME MODEL FOR TIME-VARYING SCIENTIFIC DATA

alization objects have to be combined into one visualization. As this model is independent from a specific implementation, it can be integrated in other existing visualization tools.

- Third, for the user of such a system, an easy and intuitive interaction with temporal properties in the user's domain is possible, which is based on consistent operations. While the input part of the interaction is discussed in Chapter 4, the model describes the necessary system operations to realize the user's actions.

This chapter starts with a discussion of requirements for time-varying visualization in Section 3.2. In Section 3.3, we introduce and explain our time model in detail. Section 3.4 defines consistent operations on the time model, which are applied to two use cases in Section 3.5.

3.2. Requirements

In order to allow an interactive exploration of time-varying data, a number of requirements have to be satisfied. While it is certainly possible to comply with a suitable subset of these on a case-by-case basis, only a universal solution provides enough flexibility for coping with arbitrary use cases or even combinations thereof. Along with ensuring the correctness of the depiction of a given phenomenon, the efficiency of the visualization process can be drastically increased by sophisticated data reuse schemes.

As simulated and/or measured data can stem from time spans of very different orders of magnitude, a mapping to time as perceived by the user has to be performed. Thus, depending on the context of the phenomenon under investigation, centuries and years as well as milliseconds and microseconds are scaled to manageable and perceivable time intervals of tens of seconds or minutes (*multi-scale requirement*). Besides granting the user full control over time and its progression, correct simultaneity is vital, i.e., all data displayed at any given time has to correspond to the same instant in the original data time frame [18] (*simultaneity requirement*).

In addition, the mapping of data values to time instants or intervals has to be highly flexible, as different time-varying phenomena exhibit a large variety of characteristics. Data is typically given in the form of discrete time steps, therefore a non-uniform distribution according to importance or dynamics of their content is desirable as well (*flexibility requirement*). Furthermore, both simulation results and visualization objects can consist of a mixture of static, periodic and aperiodic components. This comprises, for example, a time-varying flow field within a static environment or particle traces over multiple iterations of a periodic flow phenomenon. Data reuse by exploiting symmetries, e.g., spatial symmetry in the simulation or temporal recurrence for periodic phenomena, is vital for minimizing memory consumption. In addition, symmetry can considerably reduce the computational effort required to display and compute visualizations (*reuse requirement*).

Finally, in order to combine multiple phenomena into a single expressive visualization, the results of different simulation runs have to be mapped to a single overall time frame (*combination requirement*). In addition, any constraints regarding sampling frequency (or differences thereof) of individual simulation results have to be removed. This allows for the comparison of simulation runs with different boundary conditions as well as the composition of simulation results for different parts of a single process. In the former case, results of different simulations can be displayed synchronously for a visual comparison regardless of the respective simulation time frame. An example is the simultaneous depiction of the flow fields in an internal combustion engine for varying revolutions per minute. In the latter case, multiple simulation results corresponding to different stages of a given process can be combined into a single meaningful visualization. Examples include the concatenation of the four phases of operation for a four-stroke engine, i.e., air intake, compression, combustion, and exhaust stroke, which are typically simulated separately due to being focused on different physical phenomena.

3.3. Time model

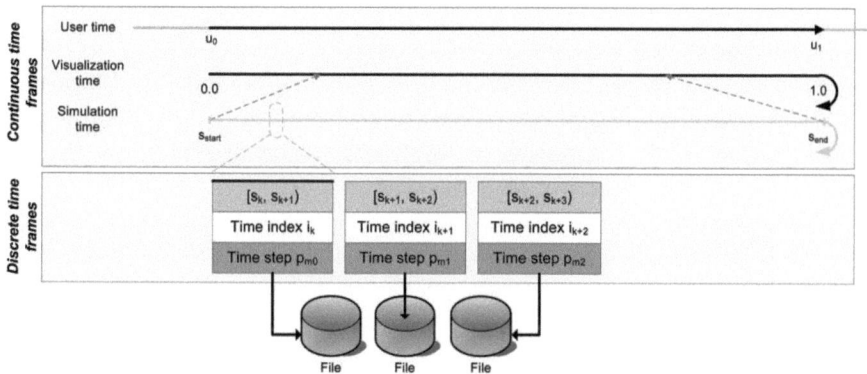

Figure 3.1.: Illustration of our time model, classified in continuous and discrete time frames. Half-loop arrows indicate a cyclic time frame. Each simulation has its own simulation time frame and discrete time frames, while visualization time and user time are global.

In order to satisfy these requirements, our time model incorporates the notion of different time frames and mutual conversion schemes, as well as flexible means for mapping instants and intervals from such time frames to specific data values. We have chosen the term *time frame* in favor over time scale or time perspective as we understand it as a frame of reference rather than a scale of

CHAPTER 3. A TIME MODEL FOR TIME-VARYING SCIENTIFIC DATA

measurement.

Different time frames are necessary, as data has different temporal properties. For example, the time frame used to simulate atmospheric processes will be different from the amount of time needed to visualize this process. In the following, we will use the word "simulation" interchangeably for all kinds of scientific data, simulated or measured.

Three time frames are fundamental for the time model and implicitly exist in most work concerning time-varying visualization:

- Of capital importance, but rarely named, is the *user time*, that is, the real-time we live in and that we perceive. It is also the time in which user reactions, interactions and runtimes are measured.

- For all time-varying processes, a *simulation time* is defined to describe the change of time in the simulated process.

- Most simulations produce data in form of discrete *time steps*, which are time instants of the simulated process. Therefore, each time step has a single simulation time instant for which it is valid.

Later, we will augment these three fundamental time frames by two auxiliary time frames which help modeling certain relations. Figure 3.1 depicts the time frames and their dependencies in our proposed time model. While the three time frames listed above form the basis of the model, two additional time frames (i.e., the visualization and time index time frame) are used for flexible interaction with the time model. This allows for mixing continuous and discrete time as well as cyclic and acyclic processes in a consistent model. If all data to be visualized is continuous (as it has an analytical description or it can be interpolated efficiently based on existing data), the discrete frames of our model may be left out.

In the following sections we will explain the time frames from top (continuous user time) to bottom (discrete time steps) (see Figure 3.1).

3.3.1. Continuous time frames

Continuous data d is defined as a function of time, that is $d = f(t)$ for some time-varying function f and a time instant t.

3.3. TIME MODEL

The first time frame is the *user time frame* $U \subset \mathbb{R}^+$. Like natural human perception, this time frame is linear, continuous, and does not allow cycles nor running backwards. In this time frame, rendering speed, interaction responses and computation runtimes are measured. Although time in computer systems is always discrete in nature, it can be perceived as continuous due to a high discrete resolution. However, images are drawn with a frequency depending on the display device. Visualizations that change time steps faster than the display frequency will not be shown correctly, as only a non-sufficient temporal resolution is available on the display.

The *visualization time frame* $V = [0, 1] \subset \mathbb{R}$ is a normalized time frame describing the complete time-varying process. As the visualization time may be cyclic, that is, the process is displayed in a cyclic way, we have to store the start point u_0 and end point u_1 (with $u_0, u_1 \in U$) of the visualization interval $[0, 1]$ in user time. We will denote the interval $[u_0, u_1]$ as the *user window*. Using these time instants, a mapping $\hat{u} : U \to V$ is defined as $\hat{u}(u) = \frac{u-u_0}{u_1-u_0}$, with a time instant $u \in [u_0, u_1]$. The time instants u_0 and u_1 change with every repetition of the visualization time, as a cyclic time frame is unrolled on the strictly non-cyclic user time frame. The length of the user window determines the time required to show the process once in a dynamic representation. The visualization time frame allows to combine different simulations with different temporal properties in a single visualization. In addition, it enables abstract interaction with the process without knowing the simulation details (see Section 3.4.2).

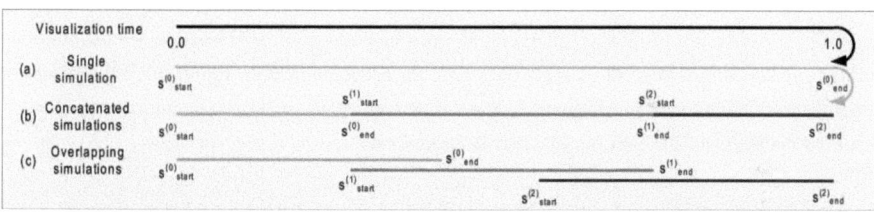

Figure 3.2.: Examples for possible relations between different simulations $S^{(0)}, S^{(1)}, S^{(2)}$ in a common visualization time frame. (a) In most cases, only a single simulation is examined. Different simulations may describe parts of a single process and are concatenated (b), if they specify consecutive stages, or overlapping (c), if they describe multiple scales.

The continuous *simulation time frame* $S = [s_{start}, s_{end}] \subset \mathbb{R}$ is the time frame used in the simulation. That means, this time frame determines the units of time used for time-varying scalar, vector, or tensor data (e.g., time-gradients, velocity, or velocity gradient). All data derived from a simulation, for instance, context geometry or annotations, are defined with respect to this time frame. It is obvious that the simulation time frame may be quite different from the user time frame in terms of measurement scale.

For each distinct simulation k the simulation time $S^{(k)}$ is associated with an interval of visualization time $[v_0^{(k)}, v_1^{(k)}] \subseteq V$ with a mapping function $\hat{v}^{(k)} : V \to S^{(k)}$ with $\hat{v}^{(k)}(v_0^{(k)}) = s_{start}^{(k)}$ and $\hat{v}^{(k)}(v_1^{(k)}) = s_{end}^{(k)}$. Several simulations or visualization objects with different simulation time frames can be

25

combined together in the shared visualization time frame. This allows for concatenated simulations or overlapping simulations (see Figure 3.2). Examples for these combinations of simulations are stated in Section 3.5.

Other names used in the literature for the simulation time frame are solution time (e.g., EnSight [25]) or data time [18]. The simulation time may have an optional associated *domain time frame*, which describes the simulation not with a time value, but a domain specific value or function. This value or function may be more intuitive for the scientist, for instance degrees crank angle for an engine piston or a date for weather simulations. In addition, granularities to describe conceptual units [3] can be interpreted as a domain time frame. A domain time frame is especially useful for communication with experts from other fields than the simulation experts, as these typically do not have in-depth knowledge about the simulation specific data such as simulation time.

3.3.2. Discrete time frames

Discrete data D is only defined at discrete time instants t_i: $D = \{(t_0, d_0), (t_1, d_1), \ldots, (t_{n-1}, d_{n-1})\}$. Scientific simulation data often comes in this form, where the discrete data d_i are simulation data at specific, possibly non-uniformly distributed time instants t_i of a simulation with a finer time resolution. We assume different discrete data $D^{(k)}$ for each simulation time frame $S^{(k)}$. Therefore, as each discrete simulation has its own discrete time frames, we will use the notation without the index k to distinguish different simulations from now on.

To provide a more flexible handling of time steps (see Sections 3.4.1 and 3.4.2), we introduce an additional *time index frame* of discrete *time indices* I, with $I = (i_0, \ldots, i_{m-1}) : i_j \in \mathbb{N}_0$. The number of time indices m may be different from the number of available time steps n. The additional indirection allows for easier reuse and reordering of time step data. This technique is often used in databases, as changing indices avoids moving or re-arranging data in memory at the cost of one indirection in main memory.

Mapping the simulation time to time indices closes the gap between continuous and discrete time frames. The simulation mapping $\hat{s} : S \to I$ is a mapping with $\hat{s}(s_{start}) = i_0$ and $\hat{s}(s_{end}) = i_{m-1}$. It is surjective, as all time indices need a valid simulation time, and monotonically increasing, as both time frames proceed forward in time.

The reversed (not mathematically inverse) function $\hat{s}^{-1}$ assigns to each time index an interval of simulation time for which the time index is valid. The codomain of $\hat{s}^{-1}$ is a set of time intervals which form a partition of the complete interval $[s_{start}, s_{end}]$. This function is a bijection, such that

3.4. TIME OPERATIONS

all time indices span the whole simulation range, and each interval is only valid for a single time index.

One example is to use a nearest neighbor mapping, that is, a time index for a time step with simulation time s_i is valid for $[\frac{s_i+s_{i-1}}{2}, \frac{s_i+s_{i+1}}{2})$. For the first and last indices i_0 and i_{m-1} no predecessor or successor exists, and at the same time the interval is invalid before s_{start} or after s_{end}, respectively. This results in half-sized intervals $[s_0, \frac{s_0+s_1}{2})$ and $[\frac{s_{m-2}+s_{m-1}}{2}, s_{m-1}]$ for the first and last time index, as we have m time indices, but $m-1$ simulation intervals in between.

The *time step frame* is composed of the simulation data output in the form of a set of discrete time steps $P = \{p_0, \ldots, p_{n-1}\} : p_i \in \mathbb{N}_0$. Each time step p_i is valid at a specific time instant s_i, which results in the complete discrete data $D = \{(s_0, p_0), \ldots, (s_{n-1}, p_{n-1})\}$. Time indices are assigned to time steps by a mapping function $\hat{i} : I \to P$. This mapping is neither injective, as different indices may point to the same time step, nor surjective, as not all time steps have to be covered. Though, the mapping $\hat{i}$ has to respect the correlation between a time step p_j and the corresponding simulation time s_j: $\hat{i}(i) = p_j \Rightarrow s_j \in \hat{s}^{-1}(i)$. That is, if the time index i maps the time step p_j, then this time step's simulation time instant s_j must be contained in the simulation time interval that is covered by i. In general, the other direction $\Leftarrow$ does not hold. This is because the simulation time interval associated to a time index can contain multiple simulation time instants, which are each correlated to a different time step. The time index however maps to only one of these time steps. This fact is required in order to enable a coarser temporal resolution (see Section 3.4.2).

The number of time steps determines the necessary size needed on secondary storage and in main memory. For all time-independent visualization techniques (e.g., isosurfaces, cutplanes or dynamic geometries), typically one result is produced for each time step. Therefore, the number of physical time steps n, i.e., the time steps which exist on a file system, determines the necessary size of buffers for different discrete visualization data.

The introduced notation is summarized in Table 3.1.

3.4. Time operations

Based on the proposed model, several consistent operations with the time-varying visualization are rendered possible. Consistency is important to maintain coherence between different visualizations of the same data. Therefore, we define a set of time operations on our proposed model which does not invalidate the produced visualizations. The operations are divided into two categories,

CHAPTER 3. A TIME MODEL FOR TIME-VARYING SCIENTIFIC DATA

Continuous time frames	
User time	$U \subset \mathbb{R}^+$
$\downarrow \hat{u}$	$\hat{u}(u) = \frac{u-u_0}{u_1-u_0}$
Visualization time	$V = [0,1] \subset \mathbb{R}$
$\downarrow \hat{v}$	$\hat{v}^{(k)}(v_0^{(k)}) = s_{start}^{(k)},\ \hat{v}^{(k)}(v_1^{(k)}) = s_{end}^{(k)}$
Simulation time	$S = [s_{start}, s_{end}] \subset \mathbb{R}^+$
$\downarrow \hat{s}$	$\hat{s}(s_{start}) = i_0,\ \hat{s}(s_{end}) = i_{m-1}$
Discrete time frames	
Time indices	$I = (i_0, \ldots, i_{m-1}) : i_j \in \mathbb{N}_0$
$\downarrow \hat{i}$	$\hat{i} : I \to P$
Time steps	$P = \{p_0, \ldots, p_{n-1}\} : p_i \in \mathbb{N}_0$

Table 3.1.: Summary of the time frame notation with notation and numeric domain of the five time frames and the corresponding mappings between time frames (denoted with a hat).

modeling operations and *interaction operations*.

3.4.1. Modeling operations

Modeling operations aid in the design and the setup of visualization applications for specific simulations. We assume that the simulation data itself—in particular its temporal characteristics—cannot be changed once it has been computed. From a visualization point of view, most simulation data can be partitioned into *static* and *dynamic* components. For instance, the casing of a pump usually defines a non-moving context for the viewer, whereas impellers or screws change over time, defining the dynamic parts of an animation. Much of the simulation topology can be exploited for visualization in order to structure and to speed up the rendering process. For example, a surface mesh can be extracted from the simulation grid and is afterwards decimated to a fraction of its original size.

Two of the modeling operations we propose target a low memory footprint and the possibility to use optimized or cached geometries for rendering. We describe three modeling operations which have proven useful for several of our applications. However, for other problem cases, there may be other operations to optimize the visualization setup.

Embedding The index mapping that is defined by $\hat{i}$ allows the embedding of few discrete time steps into a larger index scale. For example, when $\hat{i}$ is chosen as $\hat{i}_{mod}(i_j) = p_{(j \bmod m)}$ with $m = \|P\|$, $i_j \in I$, a smaller number of physical time steps can be mapped to a larger index range, for example, to exploit recurrences in the data set for cyclic processes (see Figure 3.3, both models cover twice the physical time steps). Increasing the number of time steps

3.4. TIME OPERATIONS

by interpolating data as proposed by Biddiscombe et al. [10] is achieved by insertion of time indices directing to the new time steps and adaption of $\hat{s}$ and $\hat{s}^{-1}$ to the new discrete simulation time values.

Movement In order to describe the animation of static and dynamic objects, their visualization state has to be related to the simulation time. To provide a proper mapping for the visualization state for a given time instant from S, we have to modify $\hat{s}$ to $\hat{s}^* : S \to (I, M), M \in \mathbb{R}^{4 \times 4}$. This is achieved by an additional auxiliary transform function $\hat{tr} : S \to M$ that takes as input a value of S and outputs a transformation matrix, which can then be applied to the visualization object. Static components are mapped by $\hat{s}^*$ to a constant index tuple $I = (i_0)$ and the identity matrix $M = \mathbb{I}^{4 \times 4}$. Basically the same accounts for dynamic components, however, the tuple I may consist of a number of elements and a more complex $\hat{tr}$ is needed in order to specify the state of the visualization for a specific time instant in S.

A general approach is to use a *key frame* mapping that uses discrete key frames from the simulation data. Other approaches can take knowledge of the domain expert into account, for instance, the specification of a rotational axis and angular velocity.

Events Time instants, which describe the time an event happened (e.g., a feature event or an annotation by the user), belong to the simulation time frame, as they describe events related to the simulated process. However, instantaneous time instants do not have a duration, like Euclidian points do not have a spatial size. To be observeable by a user, instantaneous events are modeled by small intervals of S enclosing the time instant of the event, with the size of the interval chosen by the user.

3.4.2. Interaction operations

Interaction operations allow to describe interactions of the user with the different time frames. This interaction with simulations and visualization objects should be possible during the time-varying visualization, to enable the user to interact with the visualized process, not only to examine it.

Human-computer interaction possesses a system transfer function that transforms the user's actions into modifications of the system's state [14]. The discussed operations are part of such a system transfer function, that is they modify the current state of the time model. Chapter 4 discusses possible input devices and interaction techniques to produce such actions.

Control The most common time operation is changing the flow of time [18]. The user can stop the flow, speed it up, or slow it down. As this just changes the user's perception of the

CHAPTER 3. A TIME MODEL FOR TIME-VARYING SCIENTIFIC DATA

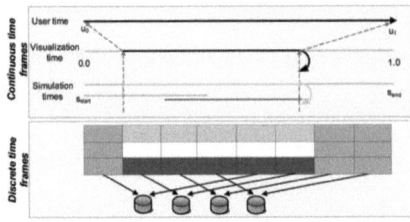 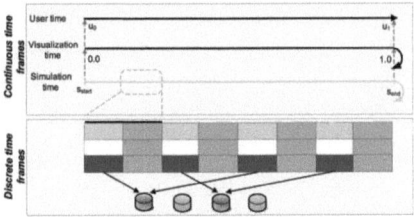

Figure 3.3.: Two of the basic operations on the time model. The time indices in the depicted models cover twice the physical time steps using an embedding operation. Left: Shown are three simulation time frames (yellow, orange, red). Selecting a subrange of visualization time selects from each simulation the appropriate sub-parts. Discrete time frames are shown for the simulation colored in yellow, only. Right: A stride of two for a single simulation excludes every second time step and therefore reduces computational effort.

simulated data, all these operations can be performed by changing the user time mapping $\hat{u}$. If $\hat{u}$ returns a constant value, the flow of time is stopped. By changing the user window length $u_1 - u_0$, the process is displayed slower or faster. Displaying a process backwards is possible by just changing the mapping $\hat{u}$ to proceed backwards from visualization time 1 to 0.

Selection For the selection of specific time instants, two time frames are recommended. Domain specialists can select a point in time by a simulation time value $s \in S$, or, if available, by the corresponding value from the domain mapping (e.g., crank degrees). By using the normalized visualization time $v \in [0, 1]$, a more fuzzy time query is realized (e.g., "somewhere in the first quarter of the process").

Range To investigate a sub-interval of the whole process, the displayed visualization time may be restricted to a subset of $[0, 1]$, which is the length of the overall process. This implies that only a subset of the whole process is displayed, which affects all different simulation data (see Figure 3.3 left). The user time mapping $\hat{u}$ must be adapted, as its codomain changes. By multiplying the length of the user window with the length of the sub-interval in visualization time, the process is displayed in its original speed.

Subset Operations on the time index frame modify the temporal properties of all time-discrete visualization objects using this specific mapping. By reducing the set of time indices, a subset of the original data is displayed. In contrast to the previous sub-interval operation, this does not have to be a contiguous subset, but may be some sort of strided subset (see Figure 3.3 right). In addition, this operation affects a single discrete simulation or visualization object only. It produces a coarser time resolution, as each time index spans a larger simulation time interval, but at the same time fewer time steps are required to be computed. By employing a non-uniform striding, "unimportant" parts of the process require less computing power. Importance in the context of temporal resolution is a topic discussed in detail in Chapter 6.

3.5. Application

In this section we will show the benefits of the proposed time model and operations for two specific use cases. We have chosen two applications for different aspects of the design consequences. The blood pump application first shows how temporal recurrence can be used to dramatically reduce the memory footprint of an unsteady visualization. Moreover, it illustrates how visualization primitives with different temporal resolutions can be integrated in one consistent depiction. The metal forming process chain application shows the benefits of the time model when creating a visualization comprising several heterogeneous simulation data sets that in combination describe a complex engineering process. Multiple simulation data sets with varying scale and temporal resolutions are combined in a consistent visualization of the overall process.

Both applications were realized using the ViSTA FlowLib [87] toolkit, into which an implementation of our time model is integrated. We provide details about this implementation in Section B.1. User interfaces that utilize the model's interaction operations are presented in Section 4.3 and Chapter 5.

3.5.1. Blood pump

As an illustrating example for the operations mentioned in Section 3.4.1, we describe the visualization of the MicroMed DeBakey VAD® (Ventricular Assist Device). Details on this data set can be found in Section C.3. The device consists of three main components: the *straightener*, the *diffusor*, and the *impeller*, as shown in Figure 3.4. These components are integrated into a cylindrical casing, which is not shown in the figure.

One impeller rotation is described by 200 time steps, i.e., the impeller rotates by 1.8 degree between every two time steps. All other parts of the geometry remain static. The simulation step size is $\Delta t = 4 \cdot 10^{-5}$ s.

As a first visualization technique, we used particle traces, seeded at the device's inlet. Assuming symmetry in the flow field after a single rotation of the impeller, the traces were calculated for a total runtime of 40 rotations as an offline process (see Figure 3.4 (b)). This results in a simulation time interval of $S = [\,s_{start},\ s_{end}\,] = [\,0.0\ s,\ \ldots,\ 0.32\ s\,]$ for the particle visualization.

CHAPTER 3. A TIME MODEL FOR TIME-VARYING SCIENTIFIC DATA

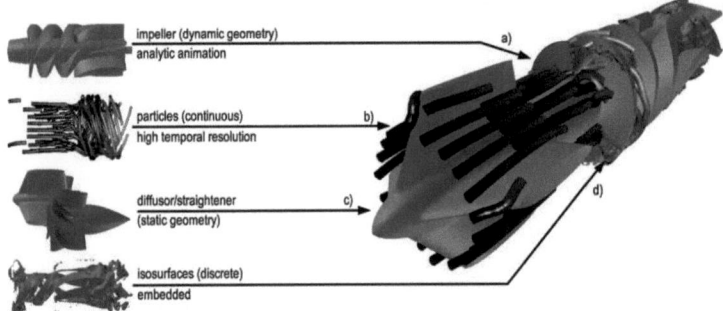

Figure 3.4.: Configuration of the MicroMed DeBakey VAD®. It is an example for a visualization that comprises different geometries, exploits temporal recurrence of the simulation, and mixes different types of data. (a) The impeller is realized as a single, analytically animated geometry. (b) Particle traces with history information are rendered over a continuous time frame. (c) Static geometries are valid over the total time frame. (d) Discrete isosurfaces are extracted, visualized, and embedded in the total simulation time frame.

As an additional, discrete visualization, we included an isosurface over low pressure. The isosurface was computed for a single rotation (i.e., 200 time steps) and then mapped using $\hat{i}_{mod}$ to 8000 time indices for the entire 40 revolutions (see Figure 3.4 (d)) using the embedding operation from Section 3.4.1. Without an additional indirection $\hat{i}_{mod}$ from time indices to time steps as described in Section 3.3.2, single time steps could not be valid for multiple simulation time intervals, which would lead to a blow-up of the data size by factor 40.

Using the operations from Section 3.4.1, the data set's context information can be reduced to single geometries. On the one hand, casing, straightener and diffusor are static pieces of geometry. Therefore, they can be modeled with a single non-moving geometry time step using the embedding operation. On the other hand, the impeller is modeled as a continuously rotating single geometry time step using the movement operation. This is implemented by an auxiliary transformation $\hat{tr}$, which calculates a rotation along the central axis for a given time instant of S based on the impeller's angular velocity. Using these mappings, only 3.3 MB of geometry are necessary in contrast to 670 MB, if the full geometry were duplicated for each of the 200 time steps.

Table 3.2 summarizes the application of the time model for this use case. The user window $U = [u_0, u_1]$ is set to $[0, 0.32\ s]$, which corresponds to the original speed of rotation. However, in the analysis process, the flow of time is typically slowed down for a detailed investigation by the user.

Using interpolation, the particle data can easily be extended to a quasi-continuous representation. Therefore, the visualization contains continuous data (particle traces, impeller) as well as discrete

	Continuous time frames	
User time	$u_1 - u_0 = 0.32$ s	
Vis. time	$V = [0,1]$	
Simul. time	$S = [0, 0.32]$	
Discrete time frames		
Part.	Isosurfaces	Geometry
Time indices -	$I = (i_0, \ldots, i_{7999})$	$I = i_0$
$\downarrow \hat{i}$ -	$\hat{i}_{mod}(j) = p_{(j \bmod 200)}$	$\hat{i}(j) = p_0$
Time steps -	$P = \{p_0, \ldots, p_{199}\}$	$P = p_0$

Table 3.2.: Time frames used in the blood pump application: Particles are continuous, isosurfaces are available for 200 time steps which repeat 40 times, geometry is either static or can analytically be rotated.

data (isosurface). The mixing of these types during the visualization can cause noticeable visual artifacts if animated slow enough. Namely, small jumps in the isosurface display are noticeable whenever the display switches to the next time index, while the continuous data changes more smoothly. Therefore, the continuously animated impeller will work very well in combination with particle visualization, but will lag after isosurfaces that are displayed using a nearest neighbor mapping for a short time as outlined in Section 3.3.2. One solution to this problem is to implement the auxiliary transformation function $\hat{tr}$ to respect a nearest neighbor mapping as well, but this will in turn cause visual artifacts with the particle visualization.

We implemented an interactive switching between different modes of $\hat{tr}$ based on user preference. Additionally, we consider the visual artifacts that result from the mismatch between interpolated particles and nearest neighbor mapped context geometry to be worse compared to the "jump" artifact from time discrete data such as isosurfaces with an interpolated rotating context geometry.

The simulation of the DeBakey pump is a good example for mid sized data sets where temporal recurrence in simulation and visualization must be used in order to work with and analyze the data. Naive approaches, such as loading all data for all rotations into main memory, are bound to fail or do not provide real-time interaction even for this moderate data size.

3.5.2. Metal Forming Process Chain

In this section we discuss the application of our time model to describe a sequence of processing steps of a metal forming process (see Section C.4). In material science, the final material properties are the result of a number of processing steps. Each processing step is simulated using different

CHAPTER 3. A TIME MODEL FOR TIME-VARYING SCIENTIFIC DATA

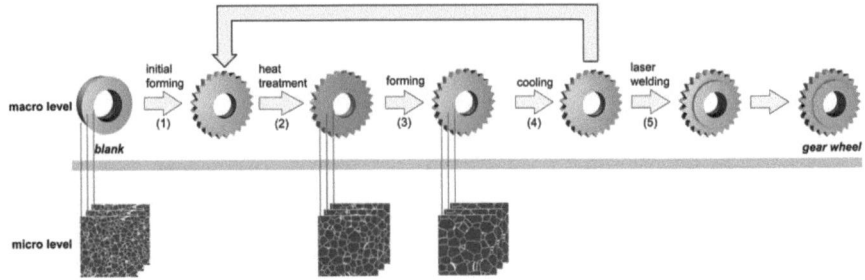

Figure 3.5.: Overview of the virtual process chain to simulate the generation of a gear wheel. Starting with a steel-alloy blank and after an initial forming process (1), the workpiece is iteratively heated (2), formed (3) and cooled down (4) again. Finally, a ring component is laser welded (5) to the work piece. The result is a completed gear wheel.

simulation tools, where each tool simulates a different aspect of the processed material. These steps have to be organized in a virtual process chain that exchanges information about the entire material and its history between the various tools.

An example of such a virtual process chain is the complete simulation of a gear wheel construction [105]. The process chain comprises five processing steps, each of which is simulated using one or two simulation tools. An overview of this process is depicted in Figure 3.5. Starting with an alloyed steel blank, an initial forming step (1) creates a gear wheel shape. In the next three processing steps (2-4), this gear wheel is heated, formed, and cooled again. Steps 2 and 3 are simulated both on a macroscopic level (overall characteristics of the entire wheel) and a microscopic level (microstructure simulation of a small region within the wheel). The heating, forming and cooling steps are repeated several times to improve material properties (a so called annealing process). In this simple example, we assume two annealing iterations. Finally, in a last step (5), a ring component is laser welded to the processed gear wheel.

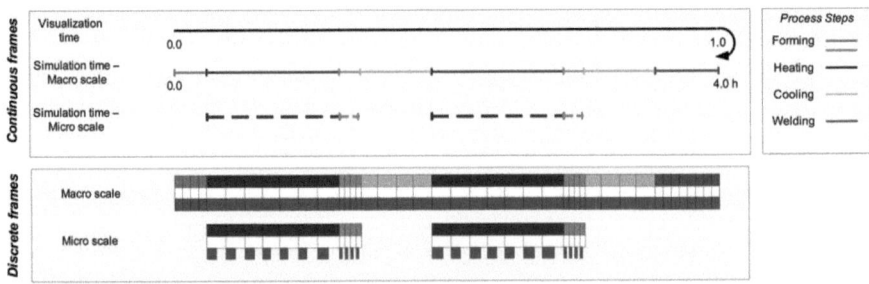

Figure 3.6.: Overview of the time frames used in the metal forming process chain. Single processing steps are color-coded, microscopic simulation data is denoted by a dashed line.

3.5. APPLICATION

Figure 3.6 shows the arrangement of the individual simulation data in the overall process. The recurring annealing steps 2-3 are not modelled using the *embedding* operation, as each annealing iteration corresponds to new time-varying simulation data. Unlike the previous blood pump example (cp. Section 3.5.1), the analyzed annealing iterations are not quasi-stationary. An overview of the time frames used to visualize this process chain are shown in Table 3.3. The gear wheel's geometry is ignored in this example, but can be modeled accordingly to the previous example.

The simulation data to individual processing steps have a varying temporal resolution. The initial forming is resolved by 21 time steps; the welding simulation data possess a temporal resolution of 360 time steps. Each step of the macroscopic annealing process is resolved with 19 discrete time steps, the corresponding microscopic simulation has a higher temporal resolution consisting of 52 time steps. As the microscopic simulation requires a complete macroscopic simulation as input data, in the sequential process chain it is simulated after the corresponding macroscopic simulation. However, in the visualization it is shown synchronously to the macroscopic data, because it describes the same process, just on another scale. The microscopic simulation consist of more than twice as much discrete time steps than the macroscopic data. Therefore, we modeled a uniform *subset* sampling of the microscopic data that corresponds to the macroscopic resolution. Consequently, nearly every second time step is dismissed.

In addition, the time scales of the individual steps vary enormously: forming takes seconds, laser welding minutes, and heating/cooling hours. More exact simulation time values for this process chain are currently not known to us. In order to display all steps in a meaningful way, a non-uniform animation of the process is required to highlight parts of the process that happen in a smaller time scale. Such an animation is realized by adapting the mapping $\hat{u}$ depending on the scale of the currently shown processing step.

Continuous time frames					
	Initial Forming (1)	Heat treatment (2)	Forming (3)	Cooling (4)	Laser Welding (5)
User time $\downarrow \hat{u}$ Vis. time			$u_1 - u_0 = 60$ s $\hat{u}$ is chosen such that the heterogeneous time scale is displayed in a scale-independent animation speed $V = [0,1]$		
Simul. time	seconds	hours	seconds	hours	minutes
Discrete time frames					
	Initial Forming (1)	Heat treatment (2)	Forming (3)	Cooling (4)	Laser Welding (5)
Time indices (Macro) Time steps (Macro)	$I = (i_0, \ldots, i_{20})$ $P = \{p_0, \ldots, p_{20}\}$	$I = (i_0, \ldots, i_{18})$ $P = \{p_0, \ldots, p_{18}\}$	$I = (i_0, \ldots, i_{18})$ $P = \{p_0, \ldots, p_{18}\}$	$I = (i_0, \ldots, i_{18})$ $P = \{p_0, \ldots, p_{18}\}$	$I = (i_0, \ldots, i_{359})$ $P = \{p_0, \ldots, p_{359}\}$
Time indices (Micro) Time steps (Micro)	- -	$I = (i_0, \ldots, i_{18})$ $P = \{p_0, \ldots, p_{51}\}$	$I = (i_0, \ldots, i_{18})$ $P = \{p_0, \ldots, p_{51}\}$	- -	- -

Table 3.3.: Time frames used in the metal forming process chain. For two processing steps (2,3) a macroscopic as well as a microscopic simulation with a different temporal resolution exist.

This example of the visualization of a virtual process chain shows the capabilities of the time model to describe complex constructs comprising heterogeneous simulation data. Both linear sequences and concurrent processes are combined, as well as processes on multiple temporal scales.

3.6. Summary and Discussion

In this chapter, we have introduced a time model for defining temporal properties in scientific visualization. The components of the model form a vocabulary for different temporal aspects of visualization objects. Based on this model, several consistent time operations for efficiency and navigation have been discussed. The proposed model is applied in several projects, of which we have described two applications as use cases.

Regarding the requirements listed in Section 3.2, multi-scale, simultaneity, flexibility, reuse and combination are possible with the proposed model. The blood pump study shows the ability to mix different time frames of a single simulation, from static geometry to aperiodic and periodic visualizations of different temporal resolution (showing the simultaneity, flexibility, and reuse requirements). The metal forming process chain study provides an example for a complex heterogeneous combination of multiple simulation data in a single consistent visualization (showing the multi-scale, flexibility, and combination requirements).

The described time model is the foundation for time-varying data structures in the ViSTA FlowLib [87] toolkit and has therefore been applied in numerous projects. While some projects did not have any special demands regarding temporal characteristics, in other projects the support of non-uniform discrete data and the movement operation have turned out to be particularly useful.

The consistent simultaneity of discrete and continuous visualizations in a single process visualization remains an open question. The same problem occurs when discrete data with inhomogeneous temporal resolutions is mixed. Whether visual inconsistencies disturb the user and if an interpolation of the underlying discrete data to continuous data or a higher resolution is feasible must be decided depending on the process under investigation.

In this thesis, the proposed time model provides the necessary formalism to describe different temporal characteristics in the following chapters. Using the model, operations on time-varying data can be described on a higher level than the actual data structures in which time-varying data is organized.

CHAPTER 4

USER INTERFACES FOR TIME NAVIGATION

4.1. Introduction

While the time model introduced in the last chapter provides a formalism to describe temporal navigation for an application programmer, a user of such a system requires a user interface to execute time operations. As stated in the introduction, a user interface that "supports all tasks emerging in the analysis process [...] in an intuitive and accurate way" (see Chapter 1) is necessary to address the interaction problem for large time-varying data. To this end, we first need to identify which tasks actually emerge in the user's analysis process. Therefore, the major goal of this chapter is to provide a taxonomy of temporal navigation tasks.

As already mentioned in Chapter 1, this thesis focuses on a Virtual Reality–based workflow. In 2000, van Dam et al. identified Virtual Reality technology as a key technology to analyze the growing amount of data [99]. They identified the improved perceptional issues (e.g., user-centered projection, stereo, wide field-of-view) and interactivity as major advantages of VR-based scientific visualization. Several case studies have shown benefits of scientific data analysis inside a virtual environment (e.g., [69, 80]). As the data sets addressed in this thesis simulate complex time-varying phenomena, we assess the benefit of a VR setting as substantial. The assumption of a VR-based workplace influences several aspects such as output representations or interactivity requirements, but it primarily dictates the feasible interaction style. Therefore, in order to navigate in time, only 3D interaction techniques are discussed here.

This chapter is structured as follows. In Section 4.2 we elaborate on a task taxonomy for temporal

CHAPTER 4. USER INTERFACES FOR TIME NAVIGATION

navigation. Based on this taxonomy, possible 3D user interfaces distinguished by the applied input device are discussed in Section 4.3. In Chapters 5 and 6, user interfaces for two selected navigation tasks are discussed in more detail.

4.2. Task Analysis

The target user group comprises simulation scientists from different fields of research, e.g., mechanical engineers, physicists, or geoscientists. Our users' demand for better time navigation techniques arose from the lack of support to perform particular temporal tasks, which became clear during several visualization sessions. We start the task analysis by describing a typical scenario with focus on user interaction concerning the time dimension. Based on this description and the analogy to spatial navigation, we are then going to organize time navigation tasks in a taxonomy.

If confronted with new data sets or unknown phenomena, the user typically starts with building up a general cognitive map of the time-varying data (*exploration phase*). At this point in time the user has not enough information to define specific targets. Hence, the user interaction is of an exploratory nature and is intended to gather information required for the following steps. Most user subtasks at this stage involve selection of animation speed or changing the shown temporal resolution to quickly focus on interesting regions.

Having obtained necessary knowledge of the data set, a user typically performs search tasks, i.e., the user tries to find specific targets along the time dimension (*search phase*). To search data in different levels of detail, temporal resolution of the discrete data set is adapted. Depending on the user's knowledge of the target, he will directly jump to a specific time instant or slowly focus on some dynamic phenomenon by restricting the visible time interval. Having found an interesting phenomena, this part of the data is typically analyzed in detail (*focus phase*). In this phase, beside maneuvering travel tasks, the user is mainly concerned with adjusting visualization parameters to investigate the phenomenon.

This characterization is in line with other classifications of the scientific visualization process. For instance, Schumann and Müller [90] distinguish the exploratory part of the analysis (here: *exploration phase*), during which users advance hypotheses, and the confirmative analysis (here: *search and focus phase*), during which these hypotheses are either confirmed or rejected.

In the scientific visualization process the user often specifies his target not only by a precise time value, but rather describes it in terms of spatial properties (e.g., "the point in time where two

4.2. TASK ANALYSIS

vortices meet"). In these cases we use the term *space-centered* task in contrast to a *time-centered* task.

In Bowman et al. [14] the term *navigation* in the context of 3D space is defined as *movement in and around an environment*. There exists a strong analogy between the navigation in 3D space and time navigation. Despite the lack of a tangible representation for *time*, navigation through the time dimension is similar to navigation in 3D space. Thus, adapting the task taxonomy of Bowman et al. at a sufficiently high level of abstraction does make sense to facilitate the analysis of time navigation tasks.

Bowman et al. classify spatial navigation into travel and wayfinding tasks. Whilst travel is a rather low-level action of navigation, wayfinding is associated with high-level cognitive activity. In an earlier work, Bowman et al. [13] have proposed a taxonomy of travel techniques. This taxonomy focuses on the following subtasks of travel: *direction/target selection, velocity selection,* and *input condition*. We use these subtasks as a basic structure for our task analysis of time travel. We prefer this classification over other existing classifications since it perfectly outlines the similarity of spatial navigation and temporal navigation. These thoughts have led to the taxonomy we propose for time navigation. [1] An overview is given in Figure 4.1.

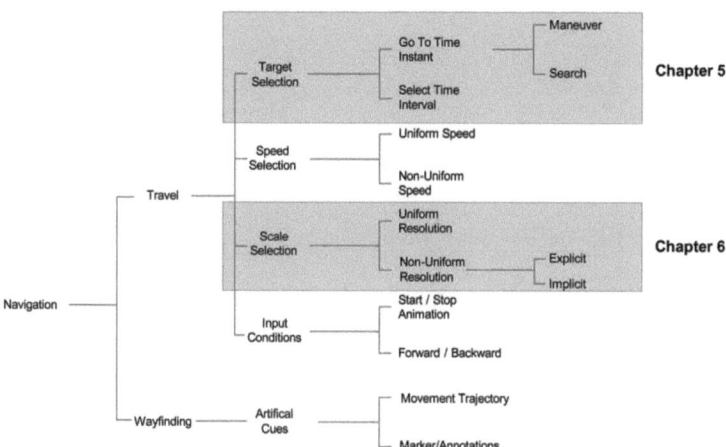

Figure 4.1.: Overview of our task taxonomy for time navigation tasks in scientific visualizations. In this thesis, novel techniques for target and resoution selection are presented in Chapters 5 and 6, respectively.

This taxonomy covers a large portion of the possible design space, but does not cover it completely. For the tasks travel and wayfinding, only a selection of subtasks is given. These can of course be further split into more detailed subtasks and technique components [12]. In the following text, we

---
[1] This taxonomy was elaborated in equal shares with Irene Tedjo-Palczynski [111].

are going to discuss the main subtasks of travel and wayfinding in more detail. Where appropriate, we are going to explain which operations on the time model introduced in Chapter 3 are necessary to model the subtasks.

Target Selection As in the original taxonomy, *target selection* refers to the primary subtasks in which the user specifies *where to move*. Single time instants and time intervals are both relevant targets for travel tasks along the time dimension. Selection of a time interval can be decomposed into the two subtasks of choosing the start instant and the end instant of the interval.

To travel to a specific time instant, two subtasks—search and maneuver—can be distinguished by the distance traveled and by the required accuracy. In *maneuver tasks*, the user investigates a specific time instant and its local temporal neighborhood. While the user will primarily adjust visualization parameters, he will also investigate changes in the temporal neighborhood. Therefore, this task is characterized by small and precise movements. Accuracy is the primary requirement, as the user accurately navigates within small time ranges. The user's goal in *search tasks* is to navigate to a specific target or time instant in the visualization. Search and maneuver target selection tasks are evaluated in more detail in Section 5.6.3. Interaction techniques that change the current time instant or interval and therefore the temporal position in the simulation are called *position control* techniques.

Time model operations: Actions to select targets utilize the *selection* and *range* operations on the time model. That is, selection of a time instant is typically specified using a simulation or visualization time value, while range operations modify the visible visualization time range.

Speed Selection describes the control of the flow of time. In the context of time navigation the best known example for this kind of task is controlling the animation speed by explicitly defining a constant value. This is an example of a uniform speed value for the whole animation. To highlight interesting parts or to skip uninteresting parts of the animation, non-uniform speed selection is also useful. Non-uniform speed selection that is not user-controlled but determined by the system based on data analysis was proposed by Wang et al. [101] and Woodring and Shen [112]. Interaction techniques that change the travel speed and therefore the rate at which the user moves through time are also called *rate control* techniques.

Time model operations: Modifying speed is a *control* operation in the time model, which changes the user time mapping $\hat{u}$. For uniform speed selection, the user window size $u_1 - u_0$ is kept at a constant value. A non-uniform speed selection is achieved by changing the window's end point u_1 depending on the current visualization time v, that is, the user window's end

4.2. TASK ANALYSIS

point is a function f of v: $u_1 = f(v)$.

Resolution Selection provides the possibility to adjust the resolution of discretely sampled time-varying data. The control over the temporal resolution is not only a trade-off between quality and computation cost, but also necessary to allow observation of different levels of details. Again, selecting a uniform and a non-uniform resolution are distinguished. While a uniform resolution needs only a single parameter to tune, non-uniform resolutions are superior in resolving interesting and uninteresting parts of the time-varying data.

Explicit configuration of a non-uniform resolution—i.e., by manual selection of interesting or uninteresting time intervals and adjustment of their discrete resolution—is a time-consuming task. Therefore, an implicit description of important and less important temporal regions by the user is a more intuitive approach. Chapter 6 addresses non-uniform subsampling based on multiple notions of importance. This differentiation is also possible for the speed selection task, but as temporal resolution is one focus of this thesis, importance-based speed selection is not discussed in this context.

Time model operations: To choose a possibly non-uniform subsampling of the available discrete data, the *subset* operation is applied on the time model. As this changes only the redirection using the time indices, available visualization data does not need to be rearranged.

Input Conditions for time navigation have similar meanings as for the spatial travel, i.e., it refers to how the travel is initiated, continued, and terminated. By using play/pause controls active travel by animation is enabled/disabled. Another input condition determines if this animation is played forward or backward.

Time model operations: Modification of the input conditions are modeled in the proposed time model using the *control* operation.

The second subtask of navigation—i.e., wayfinding—is only briefly discussed here. Bowman et al. [14] grouped wayfinding techniques into user-centered and environment-centered wayfinding support. When compared with wayfinding in 3D space, wayfinding along the time dimension covers only a 1D space. In addition, it is less substantial as arbitrary time travel is currently not possible in our world. Therefore, support for wayfinding along the time dimension should focus on providing artificial cues. We identified two basic artificial cues which are crucial to support the user's wayfinding in the time dimension. A *movement trajectory* converts the intangible movement into a tangible object to interact with. *Markers* are a standard aid of spatial wayfinding and are also suitable for a 1D environment.

4.3. 3D User Interfaces

In order to achieve a certain temporal navigation task, the user has to communicate with the computer. Bowman et al. describe a user interface as the translator between user and system [14]. Both, input to the system and output from the system need to be translated (see Figure 4.2). Slightly simplified from the original description of Bowman et al., the user's physical actions are translated by the input device into signals understood by the system. The system processes these signals—in our case using the interaction operations defined in Section 3.4.2—and generates a display representation. This digital representation is then translated by the output device into a form the user can perceive. The translations between input and output device are the software components of interaction techniques.

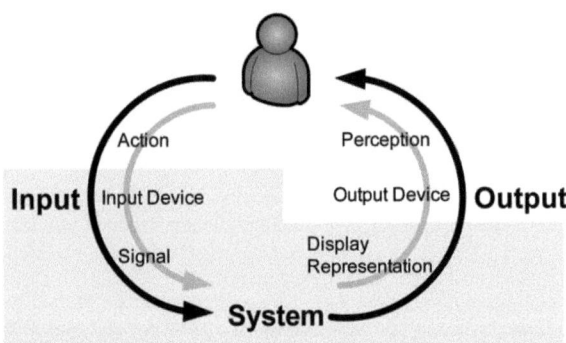

Figure 4.2.: Translation steps in human-computer communication. The yellow parts (from input device to display representation) are addressed in this section.

In this section, only components from input device to display representation are discussed. Section 4.3.1 classifies and discusses display representations for time-varying data. Sections 4.3.2 to 4.3.5 discuss several input devices that can be used for temporal navigation inside virtual environments. This section is meant to show the variety of possible 3D devices and demonstrates exemplary prototype implementations. As these interaction techniques are not novel but only adopted from state of the art 3D user interfaces, advantages and disadvantages are discussed informally only. The mentioned disadvantages and advantages for specific user interfaces are often also valid for other tasks than temporal navigation. Though, we tried to discuss the special demands on 3D user interfaces placed by temporal navigation tasks. A comprehensive formal comparison of these techniques is not reasonable, as their usability highly depends on the utilized VR-configuration and analysis task. For each interaction style, example implementations are described briefly.

4.3. 3D USER INTERFACES

Technical Realization The technical implementation of these user interfaces for temporal navigation follow a Model-View-Controller (MVC) design pattern [38]: The implementation of the time model described in Chapter 3 forms the model part, the input parts of a interaction technique act as controllers, and the output components act as views. The advantage of this construction is that only one single consistent model for all user interfaces exists. Multiple controllers can be attached to operate on the same time model. Additional views that show specific properties of the time model can also be attached. For instance, a calendar view that displays the simulation time of geophysical processes in a Gregorian calendar—using *domain time values* (cf. Section 3.3.1)—instead of measuring simulation time in days.

4.3.1. Display Representation

Virtual Reality technology provides various output devices. As the primary human channel is vision, we restrict ourselves to visual output using a "Fish Tank VR" or room-mounted display. That is, the display representation consists of stereoscopic, viewer-centered images. The display representation should be chosen such that it eases the user's cognitive task of translating the visual representation into a mental representation of the time-varying process.

Several representations are feasible to display time-varying data. For example, the field of information visualization provides several abstract visual representations of time-varying data. In this thesis only 4D scientific visualization is addressed, that is, the chosen representation should maintain the spatial (3D) characteristics of the data. Therefore, only the fourth (temporal) dimension remains as a degree of freedom to model visual representations.

Of course, in a virtual environment, the term *scene* instead of image is more appropriate, as the user can spatially navigate in the scene and modify objects. Nonetheless, we use the term *image* as this points out the correspondence to non-VR scientific visualization. Within this restriction, we identified four categories of meaningful visual representations of time-varying scientific data:

Static image A single static image displays a snapshot of the entire time-varying process. Together with the information which time instant is represented by the image, the user can manually inspect multiple snapshots to generate a mental representation. However, building a mental representation from individual still images is a strenuous cognitive task. An alternative to the classic static visualization was proposed by Joshi and Reingans [63]. By adding illustrations, dynamic information, such as movement direction or speed of tracked features, are conveyed in a single image (see Figure 4.3a).

CHAPTER 4. USER INTERFACES FOR TIME NAVIGATION

 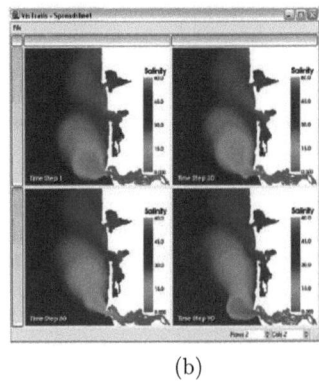

(a) (b)

Figure 4.3.: Examples of static representations for time-varying data. (a) Illustration of a feature's movement using flow ribbons (from [63]). (b) Spreadsheet view of multiple time instants at once using the VisTrails tool (from [21]).

Set of static images A selected set of snapshots is more suitable to convey a time-varying process. A popular example are comic strips, where a collection of images is utilized to convey a sequential narrative. This representation is particularly useful to provide the user with an overview of the entire process in a static scene, as several time instants are displayed at once. For instance, the VisTrails tool allows the user to compare a collection of manually selected snapshots in a spreadsheet view [21] (see Figure 4.3b). How to select a representable set of snapshots is still an open problem. For video analysis, an image-based solution was proposed by Girgensohn et al. [43]. In scientific visualization, Lu and Shen [72] proposed a method to automatically compute and display a storyboard-like overview of time-varying data. While useful for overviews, these static approaches have several drawbacks. First, a selection of snapshots suitable to the user's analysis task is crucial but not trivial. Second, collections of images require a large amount of screenspace, if the single images are shown with a reasonable resolution. Third, all dynamic information—e.g., speed—is typically discarded.

Video Videos better correspond to the natural perception of time than static images, which eases the construction of a mental representation of the time-varying process. In addition, speed can be depicted in a natural way. A video provides a changing sequence of discrete images that is perceived by a human user as a continuous motion if presented with a suitable frequency (e.g., television formats use 25–30 frames per second). Most available visualization toolkits provide an opportunity to render time-varying data into a video (e.g., ParaView [67]). From a navigation point of view, Hürst et al. remark that in continuous media such as videos only one smallest unit (i.e., one frame) is shown at a time [59], which is the major difference to other media such as text documents w.r.t. navigation.

4.3. 3D USER INTERFACES

Video or animation representations have also certain limitations. Pylyshyn found that observers can visually track a maximum of five independently moving objects at the same time [81]. The subject's performance decreases with increased speed and number of objects. Therefore, following multiple objects in a video quickly exceeds human perception capabilities.

Interactive animation When viewing rendered videos, interaction with the content is restricted to navigation in the final video. However, for an exploration of the scientific data, changing parameters or views during analysis are desirable. In an *interactive animation*, the visualization scene is constantly rendered, which enables the user to interactively modify this scene. However, this imposes high demands on the applied computational system. To enable an interactive workflow, modifications of visualization parameters have to be realized very fast. Ideally, response times of less than 100 ms are desirable [18]. While this goal is often not achievable for large time-varying data, response times of several seconds are usually acceptable [76].

The choice of a suitable representation depends on the analysis task. If the user is only interested in the last state of the simulated system and a visualization showing the interesting phenomena is known beforehand, depicting a still image is fully sufficient. However, for large time-varying data describing complex phenomena such knowledge cannot be assumed—otherwise, the term complex is unfounded. In this context, an *interactive animation* representation is preferable, as this display representation supports an explorative analysis.

4.3.2. Textual interfaces

While commonly not associated with 3D interaction, symbolic input—that is input of text, numbers, or textual markups—is useful for precise object or parameter manipulation [14]. In the context of time navigation numeric input is beneficial to travel to a specific and known location, if this location is known by its value in visualization, simulation or domain time. Textual commands can also be used to execute several navigation tasks, for instance "set time range from 0.42 to 0.66" to select a time interval, while requiring little screen space (only a single line of text).

Providing symbolic input devices in virtual environments is relatively little studied. While traditional keyboards are available for desktop VR systems, they are not applicable in fully immersive environments. Alternatives are virtual keyboards (i.e., the user presses virtual keys, which lack realistic haptic feedback) or speech input.

We assess the necessity of symbolic input for time navigation as only marginal. In our experience,

CHAPTER 4. USER INTERFACES FOR TIME NAVIGATION

important targets that are memorized by their exact numerical simulation time are rare and can therefore also be defined once, in order to be visited later with other methods—e.g., a 2D marker on a timeline. Therefore, we recommend to integrate symbolic input if possible (e.g., a traditional keyboard in desktop VR configurations, or pen-based virtual keyboards in mobile PCs), but only to augment other interaction metaphors.

4.3.3. Remote 2D GUI

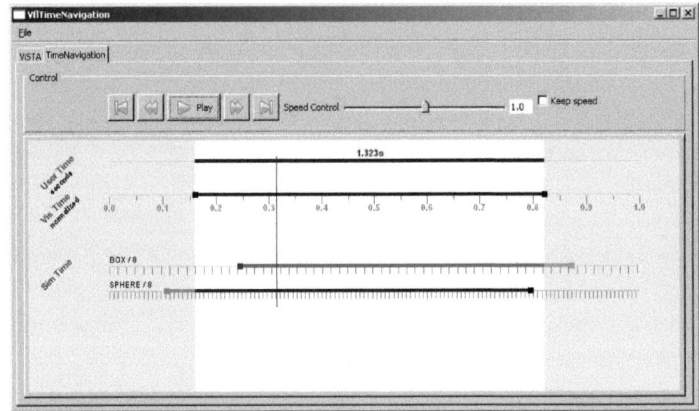

Figure 4.4.: Example for a remote 2D GUI that works as a controller for the time model from Chapter 3. Besides user and visualization time, the discrete time frames for two simulations (named box and sphere) are shown. Input conditions (i.e., play, stop) and discrete maneuvering (i.e., time step forward/backward, first/last time step) are given by VCR buttons, while relative rate control is possible with a slider interface.

Non-VR visualization applications mostly follow the WIMP (Windows, Icons, Menus, and Pointer) metaphor. Related work from document browsing or video navigation follows this metaphor, too. In order to directly benefit from interaction techniques proposed in these research fields (e.g., the Alphaslider [1]), a 2D GUI-based interaction style needs to be employed.

One way to integrate this interaction style in virtual enviroments are remote 2D GUIs on a dedicated device. The device should be mobile in order to allow application in immersive virtual environments. Exemplary devices are tablet PCs or Ultra Mobile PCs (UMPCs), as well as smaller PDAs or iPhones. The most important benefit of using a remote GUI is that it utilizes a popular interaction style with which most computer users are very proficient. Additional benefits are that such a remote GUI is independent from the performance of the VR-system (i.e., performance drops in the virtual scene do not directly influence interaction performance) and that it is suitable for general system control as well as symbolic input.

4.3. 3D USER INTERFACES

However, drawbacks when using a remote GUI are severe: the user has to carry an additional—perhaps weighty—device and possibly needs to change devices for different tasks. Remote GUIs are only applicable when the user can see the physical world (i.e., not in head-mounted display (HMD)-based systems). Input and output are spatially separated, that is, to interact with the remote GUI a focus change from the virtual scene to the 2D display is necessary.

And even the prevailing 2D slider interface has problems when used to navigate in large time-varying data. The smallest moveable unit of such a slider is constant (e.g., one pixel), which conflicts with a growing amount of discrete time steps to select. This granularity problem results in the fact that multiple temporal units are covered for a minimal slider movement. In addition, the user requires additional time to acquire the slider handle [116].

Technical Realization: The 2D GUI acts both as controller and view components of the Model-View-Controller (MVC) concept. However, as the GUI application is typically connected to the visualization application using a network, all control operations are transmitted via network to the time model. At the same time, all changes in the time model are reflected by the GUI due to its role as view component.

4.3.4. 3D GUI

Another possibility to integrate 2D GUIs in a virtual scene are adapted 2D menus and icons, that is, the 2D GUI exists as part of the 3D scene (see Figure 4.5). The 2D pointer interface is typically replaced by ray-based 3D interaction.

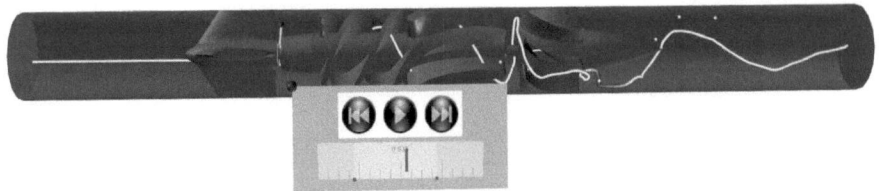

Figure 4.5.: Example for a 3D GUI: An adapted 2D GUI in a 3D scene is arranged on a 2D panel and can be freely positioned in the virtual environment.

One advantage these 3D GUIs have over remote 2D GUIs is that they require less focus change, as the focus stays within the virtual scene. The usage of free moving 3D input devices instead of a mouse is easy to learn and relatively fast.

However, they also possess several disadvantages. As the 3D GUIs are objects of the virtual

CHAPTER 4. USER INTERFACES FOR TIME NAVIGATION

scene, they can be occluded by other objects. Interaction with these menus is hindered when the visualization performance drops for complex scenes. For 2D GUIs, the utilization of free moving 3D input devices as pointers is associated with a lack of coordination due to the unnecessary degrees-of-freedom and fatigue effects. In addition, adapted 2D sliders in 3D scenes exhibit the same problems as traditional sliders. The performance using a time slider on an adapted 2D GUI shown in Figure 4.5 is compared to a novel direct manipulation interface in Section 5.6.3.

Technical Realization: The 3D GUI acts both as controller and view component of the MVC concept. For more details on the used 3D widget concept please refer to Tedjo-Palczynski et al. [98].

4.3.5. Physical Devices

Instead of using devices to manipulate controls on a screen, physical devices can also be used inside virtual environments to directly steer certain parameters. That is their control elements are directly connected to some property or action (see Figure 4.6). As a simple example, starting and stopping the animation is not achieved by using a joystick to point at the appropriate 3D widget and confirm the selection with a button, but by pressing the button directly.

The dropping prices for different kinds of game controllers (e.g., Logitech's RumblePad^{TM} or Nintendo's Wii^{TM}) makes these physical devices available for virtual environments. In addition to buttons, these devices often possess multiple analog or digital joysticks.

Figure 4.6.: Two examples of physical devices for time navigation. Left: The left-hand side elements of a Logitec Rumblepad^{TM} are used for time control. Play/pause input conditions are mapped to a single, easily reachable button, one-step maneuvering target selection is mapped to a digital left-right control (one time step backwards/forward), and speed selection is mapped to one axis of an analog joystick. Right: One axis of the isometric 3Dconnexion SpaceNavigator^{TM} is used to control speed.

4.3. 3D USER INTERFACES

Physical devices to navigate in time instead of 2D or 3D GUIs have the advantage that they do not require a visual focus change in the virtual scene, as the device is controlled via a different modality than seeing. In addition, as the device is used by touch and force, it directly provides passive haptic or tactile feedback. Recently, Swindells et al. [97] compared a mouse, a pen device, and a physical device in their usage to control visualization parameters (i.e., color values). Their study showed that the subjects spend 95% fewer visual fixations on the physical device than on the controls using a mouse or pen device. However, this did not have a significant effect on task performance.

Disadvantages of physical devices are that a special device is required and needs to be carried, and that this device is not as flexible as a graphical user interface. Only a limited number of physical controls is available on a device, so that a mapping from all possible actions to buttons is often not possible. In addition, available device controls need to be matched to interaction operations in a meaningful way, which often depends on the specific application or simulation. For instance, Lee et al. [70] found that subjects were faster using a position control jog dial or touch wheel than using a self-centering rate control scroll ring to solve navigation tasks in audio data. In general, Hinckley et al. [55] suggest that performance of different navigation techniques depends on the distance traveled. They showed that position control techniques were faster for document navigation than rate controls, however, this effect wore off with a growing travel distance.

Technical Realization: Physical devices are only used to control the central time model. While it is possible to use output properties—e.g., vibration—as views on the time model, such multi-modal interfaces are not considered here. In order to avoid input device–specific implementations, we utilize the data–flow–based approach ViSTA DataFlowNet (DFN) [7]. In this data-flow ar-

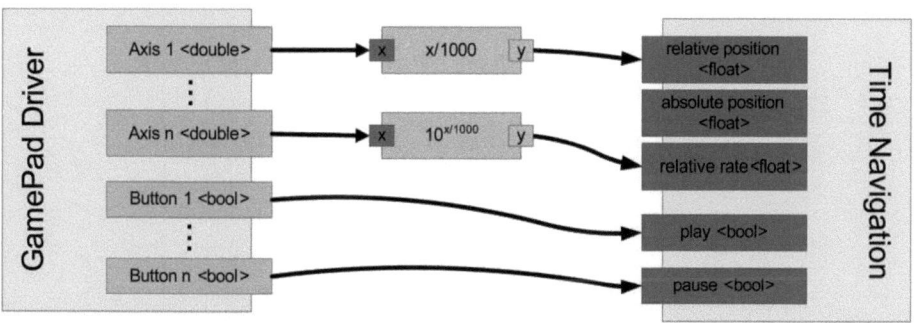

Figure 4.7.: Data-flow net for a GamePad input device. Yellow elements are nodes in the net, grey nodes transform data, blue ports are input ports, and orange ports are output ports.

chitecture, we implemented a "TimeNavigation" sink node that provides input ports to control temporal properties (see Figure 4.7). Using the network components of DFN, the output from

CHAPTER 4. USER INTERFACES FOR TIME NAVIGATION

various devices can be transformed and attached to these input ports. The benefit of this approach is that input devices and temporal operations are configured during runtime, and the addition of new input devices can benefit from existing transformations. An example for a GamePad-like device is depicted in Figure 4.7. Yellow elements are nodes in the net, blue ports are input ports, and orange ports are output ports. The GamePad driver provides several axes and buttons. Axes are encoded with a float in the range of $[-1000, 1000]$, buttons are encoded by a boolean. In this example, button 1 is directly mapped to a play animation action, while button n triggers a pause animation action. Axis 1 is scaled by 1000—rescaling possible values to $[-1, 1]$—and used as a relative position control, i.e., the current visualization time is added by the rescaled value. A value x provided by axis n is evaluated as 10^x and used as relative rate control, i.e., the current animation speed is sped up with a factor within $[0.1, 10]$; no movement of the axis maps to a speed factor of $10^0 = 1$.

4.4. Summary and Discussion

In this chapter, we have elaborated on a task taxonomy for temporal navigation in scientific visualizations. Based on this taxonomy, possible 3D user interfaces for these tasks have been discussed and exemplary prototypes have been shown. An overview is given in Table 4.1. The listed advantages/disadvantages correspond to the usual assessment of these interface types (e.g., by Bowman et al. [14]). However, we named only items that—in our opinion—influence temporal navigation tasks.

Interface type	Advantages	Disadvantages
Textual	⊕ accurate input	⊖ bad usability in fully immersive environments
Remote 2D GUI	⊕ well-known interface ⊕ performance-independent	⊖ carrying device ⊖ requires focus change
3D GUI	⊕ less focus change ⊕ easy to learn	⊖ lack of coordination ⊖ occlusion
Physical device	⊕ no focus change ⊕ passive feedback	⊖ special device required ⊖ limited number of controls

Table 4.1.: Summary of identified major advantages and disadvantages for different user interface types.

We have presented a set of 3D user interfaces, as a single best user interface rarely exists for a specific task. For instance, a user who only changes animation speed in his analysis session may prefer a physical device to control speed, while a different user who constantly changes between

4.4. SUMMARY AND DISCUSSION

speed selection and other subtasks may prefer another user interface. As a result, a suitable user interface should be employed depending on the configuration of the user's workplace, the frequency of single navigation subtasks, and individual preference. Therefore, providing a set of user interfaces that operate on a consistent time model enables a high flexibility for a large number of applications.

The presented interaction techniques are only straightforward examples that are classified by input device. Based on the well-investigated field of spatial navigation, several spatial travel techniques could be adapted for temporal travel, too. Examples include target-based techniques like the zoom-back technique by Zeleznik et al. [115], where the user automatically zooms to a selected target and after investigation zooms back to the original location.

Furthermore, the task taxonomy permits us to analyze user interfaces from existing scientific visualization tools—both VR and non-VR—regarding temporal navigation. Table 4.2 gives an overview of how and if the identified temporal navigation tasks are covered by a selected set of existing visualization toolkits. As a result, the tools we investigated provide only a limited set of interaction techniques and do not cover most temporal navigation tasks. Some tasks are only covered in a very limited way (e.g., select time interval). In particular, non-uniform tasks (i.e., non-uniform speed selection and resolution selection) are not covered at all by the visualization tools we analyzed. In almost the same manner, wayfinding is not supported. These "empty spots" in Table 4.2 suggest that temporal navigation has not been recognized as a problem. At the same time, interaction techniques and algorithms for the missing time navigation subtasks are thus identified as possible topics of emerging or future research work. For instance, recent work addresses non-uniform speed selection [101, 112]. In this thesis, Chapter 6 proposes user interfaces and algorithms to compute non-uniform temporal resolutions.

Wayfinding tasks are not intensively addressed in this thesis; only movement trajectories and markers are mentioned in Chapter 5 as wayfinding aids. However, as wayfinding is a high-level cognitive task, it may gain importance with the increasing temporal resolution of simulation data. Future research to investigate the effect of wayfinding aids on understanding time-varying data might be promising.

Tasks	ParaView 3.2.1	Visit 1.8.1	Ensight 8.0	Cloud Explorer [46]	this thesis
Go to time instant	Textual, Slider, Buttons	Slider	Textual, Slider, Buttons	Slider, Buttons	Trajectory Dragging (see Section 5.3)
Select time interval	Textual	-	Textual	Slider	Region Query (see Section 5.5)
Uniform speed	- (given by computation time)	-	Textual value depending on hardware	Slider	-
Non-uniform speed	-	-	-	-	-
Uniform resolution	Textual (by frames)	-	Textual (by time increment)	-	-
Non-uniform resolution	-	-	-	-	importance-based (see Section 5.3)
Start/Stop	VCR Buttons	VCR Buttons	VCR Buttons	VCR Buttons	-
Forward/Backward	-	-	-	-	-
Trajectories	-	-	-	numbered and colored features	particles and features (see Section 5.3)
Marker	-	-	-	-	Time Buoy (see Section 5.4)

Table 4.2.: Navigation techniques categorized by travel and wayfinding subtasks provided by four different visualization tools and this thesis.

CHAPTER 5

TARGET SELECTION USING 3D DIRECT MANIPULATION

5.1. Introduction

This chapter introduces a novel user interface that in particular addresses target selection tasks. Our goal is to ease the *interaction problem*—described in Chapter 1—by employing more accurate and intuitive interfaces. Target selection tasks are fundamental for travel inside the temporal domain as they specify *where* to move. In the last chapter we already have discussed various interaction techniques to select travel targets. The predominant time slider interface also solves target selection tasks.

The basic idea of the novel 3D user interface introduced in this chapter is to address temporal navigation orthogonal to the common time slider: Instead of manipulating an intermediary for time (e.g., a slider or a clock) and observing the spatial changes of objects caused by these manipulations, our interface is used by manipulating the spatial properties of objects, from which the system draws conclusions about the necessary temporal operations to achieve these manipulations. As an example, we enable the user to drag an identified visualization object along its three-dimensional trajectory. As each point of a trajectory is associated with a time value in the animation, this movement can be used to control time in the visualized simulation.

The proposed user interface consists of a set of three interaction techniques that address different target selection tasks: search for or maneuver to a time instant, mark and revisit a time instant, and restrict the visible time interval. For all techniques the extracted time-varying movement of visualization objects is required, which is defined by a spatio-temporal trajectory (see Section 5.2.1). All illustrating images in the following section originate from the evaluation data set described in detail in Section C.3.

To evaluate the benefit of the proposed interface, several domain scientists participated in a user study where we assessed user preference (see Section 5.6.2). For a single interaction technique, we compared quantitative measures (i.e., performance and accuracy) of this task with the common time slider interface (see Section 5.6).

In summary, the main contribution of this chapter is a novel 3D user interface for time navigation in scientific visualizations based on direct manipulation techniques.

5.2. Basic Concepts

5.2.1. Trajectories

As scientific visualization deals with representing spatio-temporal phenomena, visualized objects can exhibit motion, which can be described by trajectories. We understand a trajectory as the path an object follows when this object moves through space. The objects occuring in scientific visualization are mostly described by a discrete time frame; therefore, we assume that trajectories are also representable by discrete sets.

To establish a common vocabulary to describe the interaction techniques, we first define the term *trajectory* as it is used in the following text. Let $[s_{start}, s_{end}] \subset \mathbb{R}$ be the time range in which the simulated data is valid. This time range is in the *simulation time frame*, that is the time scale of the simulated process (see Section 3.3.1). Let $[t_{start}, t_{end}] \subseteq [s_{start}, s_{end}]$ be the life time of a certain visualization object O (e.g., a tracked feature). In this time interval, the visualization object is typically described by its discrete evolution states O_t with $t = t_{start}, \ldots, t_{end}$. A common way to depict this evolution is to show the trajectory of a specific point $p_t \in O_t$ of the time-varying object. For particle traces, this is the particle position itself. For features and geometry objects, this is often the center of the corresponding object. Then, we describe the trajectory T_O of an object O by an ordered set of three-dimensional points together with their time value $T_O = \{p^{(t)} = (p_x^{(t)}, p_y^{(t)}, p_z^{(t)}) \mid p^{(t)} \in \mathbb{R}^3, t \in [t_{start}, t_{end}]\}$. In this text, we use the equivalent notation as a set of 4D points $T_O = \{p = (p_x, p_y, p_z, p_t) \mid p \in \mathbb{R}^4, p_t \in [t_{start}, t_{end}]\}$ with $p^t = t$. In the latter notation it is easier to distinguish time instants p_t that belong to a trajectory point and general time instants t.

5.2. BASIC CONCEPTS

By interpolation of the discrete data, this trajectory can also be described by a space curve $y(t) = x$, where t $\in [t_{start}, t_{end}]$ and $x \in \mathbb{R}^3$ is a point in the 3D Euclidean space. A point on the trajectory is called a *multiple point* if there exist two time values $t \neq t'$ with y(t)=y(t'). A trajectory is a closed loop trajectory if $y(t_{start}) = y(t_{end})$. The connecting point of a loop is therefore a multiple point. If a loop is traversed more than once, all points on the loop are multiple points.

Obviously, the 3D image of a trajectory is ambiguous, as a segment in the 3D image can be traced at different speeds and multiple points are correlated to multiple simulation time instants. For instance, you can not identify from the 3D image of a looped trajectory how often this loop is traversed.

The techniques introduced in this chapter require such visualization objects with a temporal evolution that can be described by a trajectory. We identified three major visualization techniques that generate objects with a trajectory: particle tracing, feature tracking and moving geometry.

To depict the time-varying flow of a simulation, computing trajectories of massless particles is a traditional technique [103]. This visualization corresponds to inserting visible markers into the simulation which are moved according to the velocity of the flow field. Large numbers of particles can be used to convey a general understanding of the underlying flow field, such as changes in direction and velocity. See Section 2.1.1 for related work on particle tracing. To show the movement and change of identified phenomena (i.e., *features*), feature tracking techniques are employed. An overview of feature extraction and tracking techniques was given by Post et al. [79]. These techniques construct trajectories of identified features (similar to object tracking in video browsing), as well as special events of the temporal development of features (e.g., merging of two features, birth of a feature). See Section 2.1.1 for related work on feature tracking. In addition, the movement of geometry objects is known beforehand, as they are part of the simulation parameters. This includes, for instance, trajectories of rotating screws or the movement of a piston inside a combustion engine.

The extraction or computation of these trajectories from the time-varying data is not topic of this thesis, therefore we assume that already computed trajectories exist.

5.2.2. General Interaction

While the proposed interaction techniques address different target selection subtasks, some general interaction aspects apply to all of them. For all techniques, we assume the application provides at least a 6 degrees-of-freedom (DOF) input device and three buttons for state control—*select*,

CHAPTER 5. TARGET SELECTION USING 3D DIRECT MANIPULATION

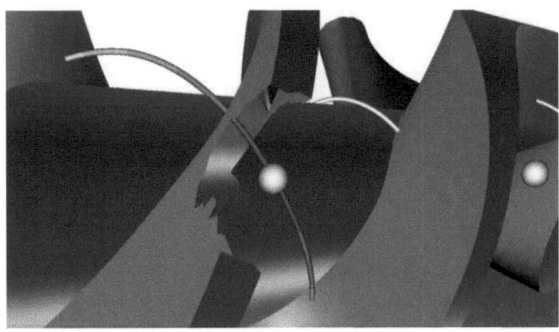

Figure 5.1.: Cut-away occlusion management. The selected point is occluded by a part of the geometry, which is cut out using an irregular jigsaw pattern.

activate and a special button for the region query. The *select* command is used to move objects by direct manipulation with the 6DOF input device while the button is pressed. *Activate* is used to explicitly create, activate or deactivate a technique, depending on the current context. The region query requires an additional *next interval* system control to switch through a set of intervals, as described later.

Selection of small or cluttered objects is hard with a standard ray-based metaphor, therefore we integrated the IntenSelect selection technique [30]. IntenSelect uses a conic selection volume and a dynamic, time-dependent ranking between objects touched by this volume. In this way, even moving, small objects—like particles—can be selected reliably.

If the simulation data contains context geometries, interesting visualization objects can accidentally be occluded by geometry. Other visualization objects are also possible distractors. To this end, we incorporated an occlusion management based on interactive cut-aways [37]. Geometry occluding a selected object is cut away with a jigsaw mask. We apply an irregular cut mask to better distinguish cutted geometry from unmodified geometry (see Figure 5.1). The choice of the occlusion management technique was made using the taxonomy by Elqvist and Tsigas [36]. A detailed argumentation for the selection of this occlusion management technique can be found in [109].

Based on these general interaction aspects, the following sections describe three direct manipulation techniques for the target selection travel subtask.

5.3. Technique: Direct Dragging Along Trajectories

In order to travel to target time instants that are defined by spatial characteristics, the user is interested in spatial positions at which some events occur. Given a visualization object with a spatio-temporal trajectory describing its development, each spatial point on the trajectory is uniquely associated with a corresponding time instant. Therefore, we transform the task of locating a specific time instant to the task of locating a specific position of a visualization object. This is done by providing the user with an interaction technique to drag selected objects along their 3D trajectory. Requirements on such a dragging technique are identified in Section 5.3.1. An interaction approach that respects these requirements is then described in Section 5.3.2.

5.3.1. Dragging Requirements

Dragicevic et al. defined four requirements for 2D dragging tasks that are also applicable to the 3D case: responsiveness, multi-scale, temporal continuity and directional continuity. A *responsiveness* of the interaction technique of less than 100 ms is required for direct manipulation [76]. The user should be able to drag object using fine controlled movements as well as fast coarse movements (*multi-scale*, see Figure 5.2 left). If the dragging movement encounters multiple points, the candidate that preserves *temporal continuity* should be chosen (see Figure 5.2 middle). If the dragging has to decide a direction, the candidate that preserves the previous direction of movement should be chosen (*directional continuity*, see Figure 5.2 right). However, single requirements often conflict with each other. For instance, the temporal continuity requirement generally prefers temporally near trajectory points. In contrast to that, the multi-scale requirement depends on the potential for large temporal jumps to reach a desired position faster. Hence, one design problem is to create a technique that offers a trade-off between these conflicting requirements. The interaction technique described in the next section tries to satisfy these four requirements while finding a compromise between them.

5.3.2. Interaction

After the initial selection of a visualization object, a *focus point* with the object's position is created (cp. Figure 5.3a). This focus point's position is displayed by a 3D cursor and it is attached to the input device retaining the current distance, such that movements of the user's input device are applied directly to the distant focus point (cp. Figure 5.3b). Using a distant cursor has two benefits compared to using the device position directly. First, manipulation of objects out of reach

CHAPTER 5. TARGET SELECTION USING 3D DIRECT MANIPULATION

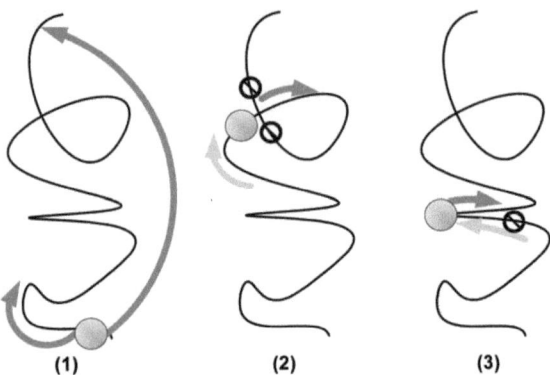

Figure 5.2.: Schematic depiction of three requirements: (1) multi-scale dragging, (2) temporal continuity, (3) directional continuity.

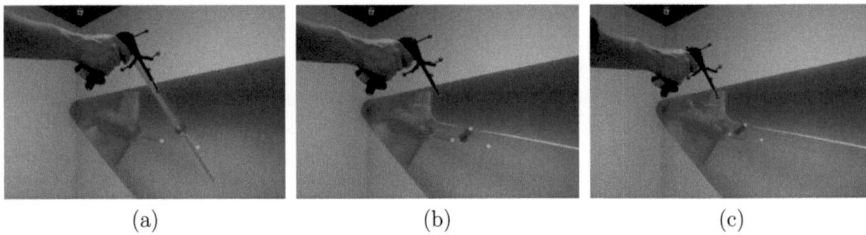

(a) (b) (c)

Figure 5.3.: Course of actions for trajectory dragging: (a) First, the user selects a single visualization object. (b) Upon selection, the object's trajectory is shown. The green rubber band connects the input position and the selected object. The input position stays at constant distance to the input device. (c) As the user moves the input device to the left, he continuously drags the object backwards along its trajectory.

of the user is enabled. Second, the real input device does not overlap with the virtual focus point, which causes perceptional problems.

Based on the focus point's movement, a new point on the trajectory is selected (cp. Figure 5.3c). The choice of the selection algorithm has a major impact on the resulting interaction technique. One possible approach is to use a closest point search on the trajectory. This is done by Karrer et al. [64], who search for the closest point in both, 2D space and time, which is described as (x,y,t). We applied this algorithm to the 3D dragging case and found the following problem: As the focus point obtained from a 6DOF device in a virtual environment is not as steady as a 2D mouse pointer, the user frequently deviates from the trajectory. This often leads to ambiguous positions of the focus point, where the spatio-temporal distance is the same for two or more candidate points.

Dragicevic et al. [33] proposed to use an adapted distance function. Based on the focus point,

5.3. TECHNIQUE: DIRECT DRAGGING ALONG TRAJECTORIES

the trajectory point with the smallest distance according to this distance function is selected. We applied this algorithm to the 3D case as follows. For a candidate trajectory point $p = (p_x, p_y, p_z, p_t)$, a focus point $f = (f_x, f_y, f_z)$, and the arc-length distance $\overline{AA_c}$ between the candidate point and the currently selected point, the distance function D is

$$D = \sqrt{(p_x - f_x)^2 + (p_y - f_y)^2 + (p_z - f_z)^2 + (k \cdot \overline{AA_c})^2} + k_{dir} \quad (5.1)$$

The arc-length distance is included to ensure temporal continuity. As time is monotonically increasing on the trajectory, so is the cumulated arc-length. Directly using the corresponding time values to a spatial point is not feasible, as time and space are expressed in different scales. The parameter k influences the effect of arc-length distance and can be described as "stickiness" of the dragging algorithm to the current time value. We assumed a higher value than originally proposed in the method to be more suitable, as we expected the freely moveable 6DOF input device to be less steady than a desktop mouse for trajectory dragging tasks. Surprisingly, in the expert reviews, all evaluators perceived a value of $k = 1$—as in the original publication—as comfortable. However, this value should be adapted to individual preferences. The parameter k_{dir} is chosen as follows:

$$k_{dir} = \begin{cases} 0 & \text{for candidate points in the direction of the current dragging motion,} \\ c > 0 & \text{else (for a predefined value } c\text{).} \end{cases}$$

This is done in order to allow for directional continuity, as movements against the current direction are penalized by a higher distance. The parameter k_{dir} should be chosen on the data set's size, as it is evaluated in data space.

The candidate point with the lowest distance according to D is then selected as the new current trajectory point, and the system travels to a simulation time value of p_t.

5.3.3. Visual Feedback

Besides a suitable distance function, the direct dragging technique needs to provide several visual feedback mechanisms. The user cannot drag an object to an arbitrary location, but the object must follow its trajectory. However, the user should not be required to follow the object's trajectory exactly. To guide the user in this manipulation task, the selected object's trajectory is displayed as a hint for possible movement (see Figure 5.4a). To be effective, this shown trajectory must be perceived in the spatial context. By drawing only 2D lines, depth information of the trajectory is strongly reduced. Instead, we propose to use 3D tubes, which provide better depth cues due to lighting and proper occlusion of each other. To ensure high frame rates even for long trajectories,

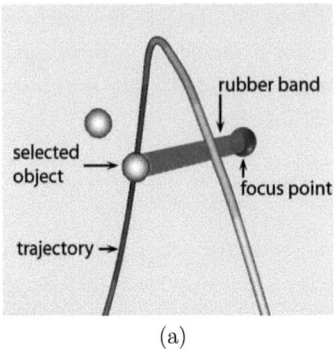 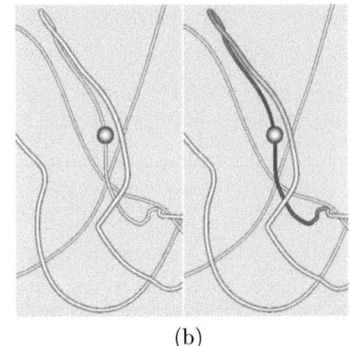

(a) (b)

Figure 5.4.: Details of the trajectory dragging technique. (a) Single components of the interaction technique. The rubber band gives additional depth information of the focus point by occlusion. (b) Comparison of unicolored trajectories and colored by temporal distance.

user-oriented billboards of these tubes are employed [88].

At the current focus position, a 3D cursor is displayed (see Figure 5.4a). First prototypes revealed that depth of the 3D cursor compared to the trajectory was badly judged. To provide the user with additional information, a rubber band between the focus position and the moved object is shown. The length of the rubber band informs the user about the distance between focus position and selected object. The occlusion of the rubber band with visualization objects provides the user with additional depth cues (see Figure 5.4a).

Even a single trajectory might exhibit complex structures, resulting in intricate "ball of yarn" views. An example is provided in Figure 5.4b. This does not only impede the user's understanding of the trajectory, but also the task of dragging along the trajectory, as the local position can also be intricate. To counteract this problem, we color the hint trajectory according to the temporal distance to the selected point. That is, a point on the trajectory temporally closer to the current selected point gets a more noticeable color than a point farther away in time. This highlights contiguous segments, which eases the perception of the local neighborhood around the selected point. Of course, the drawback of this visual hint is that no other information related to the analysis can be mapped to the trajectory's color (e.g., the object's velocity magnitude). Therefore, we implemented this visual hint as optional.

5.3.4. Technical Realization

For a fast search for the best candidate with respect to the distance function D, we employ a k-d-tree. To reduce the memory footprint for a large number of trajectories, the tree structure is built upon initial selection of a trajectory. Each trajectory point is stored by four components: the three spatial components p_x, p_y, p_z and its accumulated arc-length value from the beginning of the trajectory. This allows to encode the stickiness parameter k into the arc-length value stored in the k-d-tree. Changes of parameter k are then taken into account with each new selection of a trajectory. However, the directional parameter k_{dir} can not easily be included in the search tree, as it changes with every direction change. Therefore, this parameter is evaluated on an intermediate set of candidate points from the k-d-tree search. Based on this last evaluation step, the closest candidate point according to the distance function D is selected.

5.4. Technique: Time Buoy

Providing cues for significant events in the time-varying data supports wayfinding in navigation tasks. To mark temporal properties of an event, it is sufficient to set a mark on the 1D timeline. However, in the analysis of spatial data marked events are often correlated with a spatial region where this event has occured. Therefore, the *time buoy* represents a marking mechanism for both, space and time. Besides wayfinding tasks, the time buoy can also be used for target selection tasks to return to previously marked positions or time-instants.

5.4.1. Interaction

On request, a buoy-like marker—consisting of a colored flag and a buoy body—is created that marks the current time instant and can be positioned in space (see Figure 5.5). The spatial position of the marker can be changed by selecting the base of the buoy and directly moving the marker. To change the temporal position of the marker, the user has two options:

First, to mark positions that are not on a trajectory, the user presses the activate button to turn the time buoy into in a special "time-traveling" state. While in this state, the time buoy is half-transparent and adopts the current time, as it is changed by other time navigation methods. When deactivating this state, the time buoy remembers the last time value.

Second, to mark positions which belong to a trajectory, the buoy can be directly attached to a trajectory point. When in close proximity to a trajectory, the time buoy is attached to the spatially nearest point $p \in \mathbb{R}^4$ of the current trajectory. The connection between buoy and trajectory is made visible to the user (see Figure 5.5). The buoy's time value is set to the connected trajectory point's time value p_t. By moving the buoy away from the trajectory far enough—that is, above a predefined threshold—, the connection is deleted.

61

CHAPTER 5. TARGET SELECTION USING 3D DIRECT MANIPULATION

Besides representing markers for certain events, time buoys can be used to directly go to the time instant of the event (i.e., for target selection tasks). By selecting the flag of the buoy, the user moves to the point in time represented by the time buoy. Using these buoys, AB-comparisons for time instants—i.e., comparing a visualization in alternating time instants—are made easy. Sequences of events can be marked by time buoys and by selecting the buoys' flags, the user can jump through this sequence.

5.4.2. Visualization

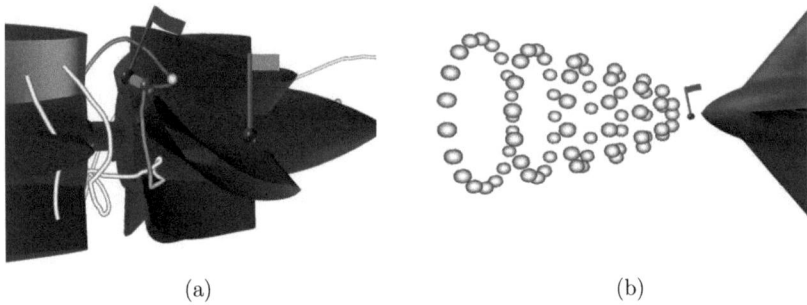

(a) (b)

Figure 5.5.: Time buoys marking spatio-temporal positions. (a) The red buoy is attached to a trajectory (yellow connection), and as the current time value is close to the marked one, the flag is active. The light green buoy is inactive. (b) The active green buoy marks the trajectory-independent event that the first particles reach the straightener.

The spatial position is represented by the buoy's spherical floating body. Whenever the marked time is active, the time buoy is animated like a floating buoy in heavy waves. The marked time is encoded as motion, since motion is well noticeable even in peripheral vision; this is important for room-mounted displays, where the user is possibly surrounded by the data. In order to inform the user that a marked event is close, the animation is activated if the current time is within Δt of the marked time instant. At the same time, the distance to the marked event is encoded in the amplitude of the buoy's swinging motion. For the current time value $t_{current}$ and the marked time instant t_{marked}, the normalized amplitude A is given by $A = 1 - \frac{|t_{current} - t_{marked}|}{\Delta t}$, that is the buoy swings faster close to the marked time instant and very slowly when the distance approaches Δt. However, as the temporal position of a buoy is not directly perceivable by the user, information about the marked time instant has to be displayed to the user. On selection of a buoy, the marked time instant and position is displayed as text. The marked time instant is additionally shown on a 1D timeline (e.g., on the 3D GUI described in Section 4.3.4). This provides the user with an overview of the temporal positions of all time buoys, while neglecting the spatial positions.

5.4.3. Technical Realization

As the time buoy represents a marking mechanism, no considerable computational effort is necessary. The most costly operation is the check for closeness to the selected trajectory, which is handled by the k-d-tree point search of the trajectory dragging technique.

5.5. Technique: Region Query

Selecting a time interval to restrict the range of the animated sequence helps focusing on interesting time-varying phenomena. Often interesting phenomena lie inside a known spatial region. For moving visualization objects, this region can be visited multiple times, depending on the underlying flow. Using a time slider interface, the course of action comprises manipulation of the slider range until the observed objects move through the desired region only. Instead of restricting the time range to time intervals where objects reside in a spatial region, we propose the other way round, that is, to specify the target spatial region and then to compute the time intervals, in which this region is visited.

5.5.1. Interaction

To specify the target region, we provide the user with a box-shaped widget to describe a rectangular region. In order to create such a box, the user stretches out the box's diagonal while pressing the activate button (see Figure 5.6a). Although directly drawing a box inside a virtual environment is very intuitive, defining the box's extents in this way is often inaccurate. Therefore, an existing box can be reshaped by selecting a single face and directly dragging this face along the corresponding box's axis (see Figure 5.6b). Additionally, the user can select the whole box and reposition it freely. Throughout this process the previously defined box remains visible for reference. This combination of coarse but intuitive creation and iterative refinement enables the accurate definition of a spatial region inside a virtual environment even with freely moveable input devices. Details on this drag box widget can be found in Hentschel et al. [54].

Given a set of trajectories for all moving objects and a box widget describing the target region, we compute the spatio-temporal intersection of these objects and the specified spatial region. That is, for each object O (where O_t is the spatial description of the object at time instant t) and a spatial rectangular region R we compute the discrete set of time instants $I_O = \{t \mid O_t \cap R \neq \emptyset\}$ during which the object touches or resides within the region. Of course, this approach is not restricted

63

CHAPTER 5. TARGET SELECTION USING 3D DIRECT MANIPULATION

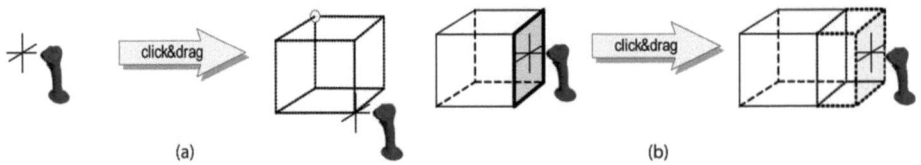

Figure 5.6.: Two of the three possible actions of the drag box widget (from [54]): dragging a new box in 3D space (a) and refining a single face and therefore a single box axis (b).

to a rectangular query region—e.g., the same approach is possible using a spherical widget.

Based on the discrete temporal resolution of the object, these time instants I_O are transformed into a set of disjunct time intervals $\bar{I}_O = \{[t_s, t_e] \mid \forall t \ t_s \leq t \leq t_e : t \in I_O\}$ that envelop these time instants (i.e., $t \in I_O \Leftrightarrow t \cap \bar{I}_O \neq \emptyset$ holds). We combine these interval sets $\bar{I}_O$ for all objects and determine the minimal set of intervals $\bar{I}$ spanning the same time ranges as the union over the sets $\bar{I}_O$. The result is a set of time intervals $\bar{I}$, during which movement inside the query region occurs. We call an element of this minimal set an *active interval*. By using the next interval button (see Section 5.2.2) on an active region, the user can switch through the set of active intervals that are shown in an animation.

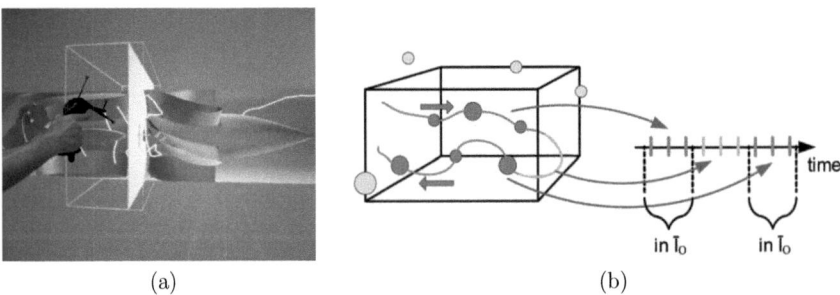

Figure 5.7.: Interaction and effect of the region query technique: (a) After having selected a spatial region using the box widget, the user refines one face. (b) Points inside the query region are shown in orange, points outside in light blue. On the timeline, the trajectory points that reside inside the region correspond to two active time intervals, separated by a time interval during which the trajectory is outside the query region.

An example is depicted in Figure 5.7. For the data set described in Section C.3, the user selects using the box widget the transition region between impeller and diffuser (see Figure 5.7a). Figure 5.7b shows a sketch of the situation: a single trajectory passes through the query region two times, resulting in two active intervals separated by a time interval during which the trajectory is outside the query region. Figure 5.8 shows how the sets $\bar{I}_O$ of three objects are combined to the single set of active intervals.

5.5. TECHNIQUE: REGION QUERY

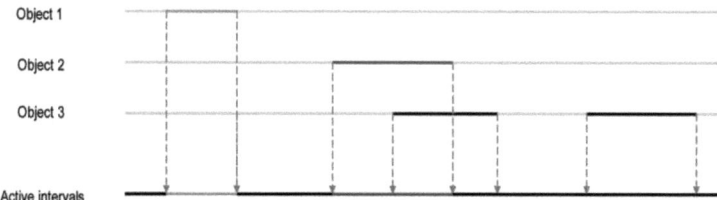

Figure 5.8.: Example of active intervals obtained from three visualization objects. Each of the three objects has a set of time intervals (colored lines) within its lifetime (grey line), in which it resides in the query region. These intervals are combined to three disjunct active intervals. During each active interval, the region is visited by at least one object.

5.5.2. Visualization

Besides the visualization of the drag box widget, additional information for the currently active interval are displayed. That is, on selection of an active interval, the set of trajectories that pass the query region in this interval is shown. In order to depict the relation of active intervals, these intervals are displayed on a 1D timeline legend for reference (e.g., see Figure 5.8). Such an additional 1D depiction is reasonable, as it is the commonly used visualization of interval data. By selecting the 1D interval representations, the user can travel between active intervals. Consequently, the visual range is restricted to the selected interval.

5.5.3. Technical Realization

The efficient search of active intervals depends on the shape of the query region and the shapes of the visualization objects. For the example of the DeBakey VAD, we restricted the region query technique to particle traces, only. That is, the visualization object at each time instant can be described by a single point, which is why we employ a k-d-tree data structure. When implementing the region query technique for objects with spatial extents, other spatial data structures such as an R-tree would be more appropriate.

We employ a single k-d-tree that stores the union of all trajectory points from all trajectories using their three spatial components p_x, p_y, p_z. Using this tree, all points that lie spatially inside the query region are retrieved. For a spherical or box-shaped query widget, the k-d-tree provides efficient search algorithms. The resulting points are sorted by their time value p_t and partitioned into disjunct intervals, which already are active intervals. The interval sets $\bar{I}_O$ for each object are not explicitly created.

Using the region query technique, the user can easily focus on time-varying phenomena inside a spatial region of interest.

5.6. Evaluation

To assess the usability of our 3D user interface, we combined several evaluation techniques. During the design process, we conducted expert reviews (results not shown here), which were especially helpful to find hidden design flaws and errors. We conducted two user studies, one study assessing user preference for all techniques (see Section 5.6.2) and a detailed comparison for a selected technique (see Section 5.6.3). Two separate studies were conducted to keep the required time for a single study within an acceptable limit of one hour. Both studies were carried out in a 5-sided CAVE-like environment using an A.R.T. Flystick as input device. All participants belonged to the target user group, i.e., all had experience in simulation science, and ranked their experience in simulation science on a 5-point scale (1 = no experience, 5 = expert) with a median value of 4. To create a strong reference to scientific visualization, we designed tasks inside a real-world visualization application. However, the tasks themselves did not incorporate domain-specific knowledge (i.e., tasks such as "What effect has shear flow on hemolysis?"). To analyze the proposed method we selected the visualization of the MicroMed DeBakey VAD® (Ventricular Assist Device), because this visualization contains a set of non-trivial trajectories, that are larger and more complex compared to existing trajectories from the available other data sets. See Section C.3 for details on the DeBakey VAD.

5.6.1. Technical Evaluation

Here, we used a pre-computed set of 75 pathlines that follow 36 revolutions of the impeller. The average length of a trajectory was 4900 points, the total of 75 pathlines comprised 325,621 points. While the longest pathlines had 5200 points, several trajectories needed less revolutions to leave the blood pump or terminated earlier due to low velocity. All measurements were done on a PC with a Intel Core2 Quad processor at 2.83 GHz, equipped with 4 GB main memory.

For the trajectory dragging technique, the k-d-tree is built on-the-fly, whenever a particle is newly selected. For this data set, building the k-d-tree took on average average 1.86 ms (standard deviation 0.18 ms). To search a new trajectory point according to the given distance function took on average 0.19 ms (standard deviation 0.008 ms). These numbers show that a good deal larger trajectories can be handled by the trajectory dragging technique within the desirable response time

5.6. EVALUATION

of 100 ms. Of course this measurements were collected for a specific implementation and hardware, only. Though, the numbers represent achievable results on a current computer system.

To evaluate the region query technique, queries with different query sizes were executed. Table 5.1 shows query runtimes for box-shaped region queries with a side length of 5 % to 100 % of the data set's side lengths. Querying 100 %, that is the full data set, was done for comparison purposes, as

Region query size	avg. runtime
5 %	14.7 ms
10 %	17.5 ms
25 %	31.4 ms
50 %	36.4 ms
100 %	116.4 ms

Table 5.1.: Average runtimes for the region query techniques for regions of varying size relative to the data set's size.

this query trivially returned the full time interval. For the full query, runtimes above an immediate response time of 100 ms were measured. In all other cases, response times of the region query technique were clearly below 100 ms. But in spite of this, these results show that for larger trajectories or a larger number of trajectories, an immediate response time of 100 ms is easily exceeded. We argue that, as the user does not have a direct correspondence between input action (i.e. drawing a box) and result (i.e., a set of active intervals that restrict the animation), such an immediate response is not essential. The user will anyway need additional time to step through the intervals and start the animation. For these reasons we argue that a response time within two seconds will also be acceptable [76] for this interaction technique.

5.6.2. Questionnaire

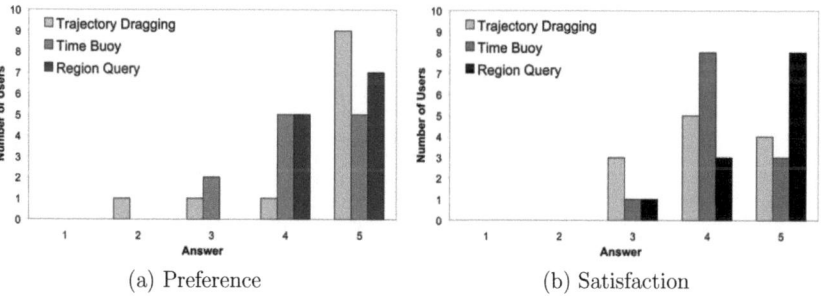

(a) Preference (b) Satisfaction

Figure 5.9.: Participants rated on a 5-point Likert scale if they preferred a direct manipulation technique to the time slider interface (1=strongly disagree, 5=strongly agree) as well as overall satisfaction with the technique (1=frustrating, 5=satisfying).

In a user study, all techniques were evaluated concerning qualitative aspects of the interface. The participating domain scientists explored the user interface given several specific goals. In a questionnaire, we inquired aspects of the interface's usability.

Twelve simulation scientists (2 female, 10 male) between 19 and 30 years of age (mean 25.8) were recruited to compare the interaction techniques.

Procedure — After an introduction into the visualization of the data set and a brief explanation of the time slider and the four new techniques, the participants explored all techniques in a free training phase of at most 10 minutes. Thereafter, they were given four different tasks, which they had to solve with both the time slider and an appropriate new technique in varying order. Finally, the participants answered a questionnaire to rate their experiences on a 5-point Likert scale. The experiment took half an hour on average per participant.

Qualitative Results — Figure 5.9 depicts the subjects' responses to two questions: "I would prefer the technique to the time slider interface for the execution of the task" (Figure 5.9a) and "Rate your overall satisfaction with the technique" (Figure 5.9b). Most subjects clearly preferred the direct techniques to the common time slider interface (median 5), and perceived the overall satisfaction using these techniques as quite high (median 4). Operation of the time buoy widget was also rated high: selection of an existing buoy was rated easy (median 4) and connecting a buoy to the current trajectory as very easy (median 5). All three operations of the drag box widget—defining a new box, resizing one face, and moving the whole box—were all rated very easy (median 5). All techniques were also rated as very intuitive (median 5), and the subjects did not state any problems learning the functions of the new techniques. No participant reported any signs of sickness during the experiment.

5.6.3. Comparative Evaluation

For a detailed comparative evaluation, we selected the trajectory dragging technique. We compared the trajectory dragging to the linear time slider commonly used in visualization applications. Eight simulation scientists (2 female, 6 male) between 22 and 29 years of age (mean 26.0) were recruited to compare the interaction techniques.

Procedure — After an introduction to the system, a free training phase of at most 10 minutes, and 5 test tasks, each participant conducted a total of 80 tasks using both interaction techniques (*independent variable*) — 60 tasks for this study and 20 tasks for another study [109]. The experiment took one hour on average per participant. These 60 tasks consisted of a equal mixture of *search, maneuver* and *moving target* tasks with varying distances to travel. For both, *search*

5.6. EVALUATION

and *maneuver* tasks, the spatial target to navigate to was non-moving. We defined *maneuver* tasks as navigation tasks with a maximal distance of 10 % of the data set's temporal resolution, and *search* tasks as all tasks above 10 %. In *moving target* tasks, the navigation target slowly moved on a straight line in one direction. The latter tasks were included in this study to represent user goals that incorporate interaction of moving visualization objects (e.g., "When do these two vortices meet?").

All tasks were space-centered, for instance "Position a visualization object on a target plane!". In all tasks, the start and target positions of visualization objects were not hidden by geometry, to prevent a disadvantage of the slider technique, which has no occlusion management. Maximum duration for a task was set to 15 seconds.

Two values were measured for each task (*dependent variables*), the task performance time in seconds, and the accuracy of the subject's navigation. Accuracy is measured as absolute error in the normalized time scale from 0 % to 100 %. The reported absolute values are quite small, though it should be noted that an absolute error of 0.019 % corresponds to one discrete time step. Tasks were carried out using a within-subjects design, the order of execution for trials was varied using Latin squares. Independent variables were interaction technique (time slider vs. trajectory dragging). Dependent variables were task completion time and accuracy of executed task. Participants were instructed to complete the tasks as fast and as accurately as possible. Hence, outliers in the data above 15 seconds performance time and above 10 % absolute error were removed. The observation of subjects during the study and recorded data suggest the assumption, that these outliers result from erratic behavior of the subjects, that is performance time outliers are coupled with high accuracy, while accuracy outliers are coupled with fast performance times.

Two hypotheses were tested: users are both faster (*H1*) and more accurate (*H2*) with 3D trajectory dragging compared to a time slider for space-centered search and maneuver tasks.

Quantitative Results — We evaluated the task performance and accuracy data and tested the hypotheses using paired Student's t-tests. The results are depicted in Figure 5.10. Subjects were on average 25 % faster with the trajectory dragging than using the time slider (p=0.01, t(7)=2.967). Concerning accuracy, subjects were on average 48 % more accurate when using direct trajectory dragging (p=0.019, t(7)=2.537). Thus, we accept both hypotheses *H1* and *H2*.

In the following, the recorded performance and accuracy data is evaluated in more detail. Figure 5.11 shows a histogram of ocurred absolute error values. This histogramm clearly shows that subjects using the trajectory dragging (b) frequently achieved very low error rates (i.e., high accuracy). In contrast, the distribution of error values using the time slider (a) is much more broader. Figure 5.11b shows, that accuracy outliers can occur in the usage of the trajectory drag-

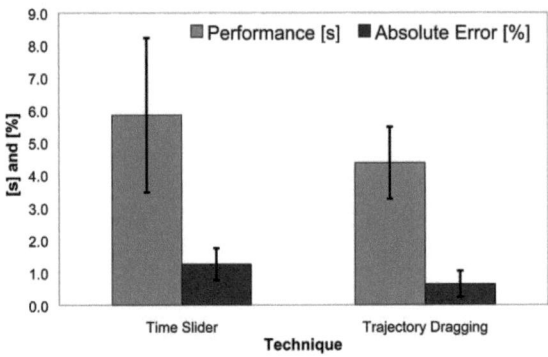

Figure 5.10.: Comparison of task performance and absolute task error for the time slider and the trajectory dragging technique.

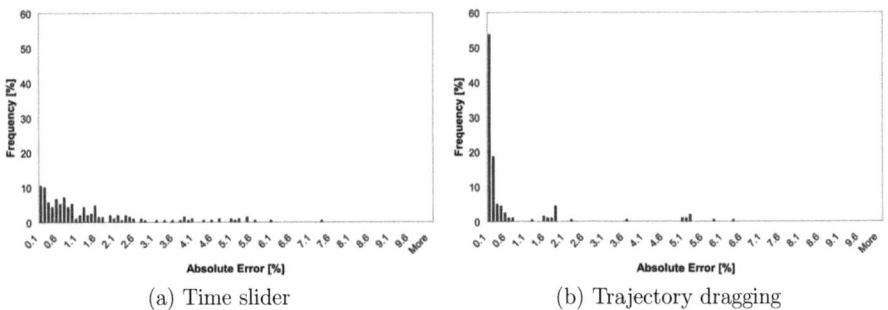

Figure 5.11.: Histograms of recorded accuracy data (measured in absolute error) for all subjects using (a) the time slider and (b) the trajectory dragging.

ging technique (e.g., peaks at 2 % and 5 %), which shows that there is room for improvement of the interaction technique. For task performance data, the histogram shows no such obvious pattern.

Table 5.2 shows a comparison of performance and accuracy differentiated by the task's type (i.e., maneuver, search, and moving targets). Subjects performed maneuver tasks faster than both search tasks for fix and moving targets, that is subjects traveled faster to closer targets. This was expectable, as target distance is often directly correlated to task performance (e.g., Fitt's Law). Using the trajectory dragging technique, users performed worst (i.e., slow and inaccurate) in search tasks compared to maneuver tasks and tasks with moving targets. This can be explained by the larger target distance, as the worsening is in line with the time slider performance results. However, while using the time slider for search tasks nearly doubles the average absolute error compared to maneuver tasks, using the trajectory dragging the average absolut error increases by only 17 %, that is trajectory dragging allows for more accuracy even for distant targets.

Task	Technique	Task performance Mean	Std.dev.	Absolute error Mean	Std.dev.
Overall	Time slider	5.85 s	2.38 s	1.258 %	0.489 %
	Traj. dragging	4.37 s	1.1 s	0.642 %	0.402 %
Maneuver	Time slider	4.61 s	2.25 s	0.897 %	0.207 %
	Traj. dragging	3.41 s	0.79 s	0.502 %	0.199 %
Search	Time slider	7.03 s	3.78 s	1.77 %	0.702 %
	Traj. dragging	5.48 s	1.45 s	0.579 %	0.214 %
Moving targets	Time slider	7.26 s	1.89 s	1.292 %	0.995 %
	Traj. dragging	4.95 s	0.94 s	0.402 %	0.404 %

Table 5.2.: Comparison of the trajectory dragging technique with a time slider interface differentiated by task type. Measures are performance time and absolute error.

While trajectory dragging beats the time slider in both performance and accuracy for all three types of tasks, the difference is largest for tasks involving moving objects: Subjects performed on average 31 % faster and 68 % more accurate using the direct manipulation technique than using the slider when they had to travel to a changing target. From that we conclude, that trajectory dragging is especially useful to navigate to events where moving visualization objects interact with each other.

5.7. Summary and Discussion

We have presented a novel 3D user interface for time navigation in scientific visualization. By directly interacting with the visualization objects, a user can move through time, focus the animation interval, and insert spatial cues for wayfinding.

In the evaluation of this task-specific 3D user interface, simulation scientists rated it intuitive and preferable to the commonly used time slider for space-centered tasks. A more detailed evaluation of the trajectory dragging revealed that users were both faster and more accurate using direct manipulation using the trajectory dragging for active travel, in particular when traveling to moving targets. The region query technique received the highest ratings from all techniques, and was emphasized by single subjects as especially useful. While users clearly preferred the trajectory dragging, reported satisfaction for this technique showed a high variance. In addition, single users had problems applying this technique to solve the given task, and outliers in the accuracy performance occured. For these reasons, we identified this technique as a focus of future improvements and research.

CHAPTER 5. TARGET SELECTION USING 3D DIRECT MANIPULATION

While most subjects preferred the new spatial techniques, some subjects made clear that they would like to use it in combination with the time slider. This affirms the initial design goal, that this interface is meant to augment, not replace the common time slider interface.

One limitation of our approach is, that not all visualizations of scientific data sets possess objects with extracted trajectories (e.g., as only the color on a fixed object changes). However, from the obtained results, we conclude that augmenting the traditional time slider interface with a more direct 3D interface for temporal navigation provides a clear benefit for the analysis of time-varying scientific data.

Due to the positive feedback and good results of the direct manipulation techniques, we plan to port this 3D user interface to a non-VR desktop workplace. The renunciation of stereoscopy and the application of a 2D input device like a mouse will require major changes and a new evaluation of the interaction techniques. However, if successful, this will provide a major benefit for domain scientists analyzing their data in daily work.

CHAPTER 6

IMPORTANCE-BASED TEMPORAL SUBSAMPLING

6.1. Introduction

Currently, the standard approach to visualize time-varying data still is to apply known time-independent visualization techniques (cf. Chapter 2) to all time steps in order to generate individual frames for a continuous animation. Especially for an interactive exploration of the data, domain scientists often rely on a set of traditional visualization techniques (e.g., cutplanes or glyph-representations) that are employed in this way.

However, the analysis of scientific data sets by application of time-independent visualization techniques is hindered by the high temporal resolution of the target data sets (the *computation problem*, see Chapter 1). Given only limited memory or processing power, the user is restricted to select only a subset of the entire temporal resolution for visualization. In addition, the straightforward rendering of a visualization comprising all discrete time steps results in overly long animations or videos. Especially in an interactive exploration scenario, where the scientist continuously varies parameters, the examination of an animation running several minutes is not appropriate.

Therefore, using a subset of the available discrete data is inevitable. A common approach is to use a uniform subsampling of the time-varying data. Though, this often does not resolve temporal important parts of the data adequately, and at the same time resolves less important parts with an unnecessary high resolution.

The goal of this chapter is to compute a non-uniform sampling for a given temporal resolution, which adapts itself to the temporal importance of time-varying data—i.e., more important data is resolved using a high temporal resolution, while less important parts are shown with a minimal resolution only.

In order to distinguish different degrees of importance, we introduce the term *temporal importance* and classify different concepts of importance (see Section 6.2). We will give examples for different temporal importance functions which are obtained from existing visualization techniques as well as direct user input (see Section 6.3). Ultimately, importance should be defined by the user in the context of the current analysis.

Multiple importance functions are necessary to highlight different aspects of a time-varying process. As these functions are possibly conflicting with each other, we formulate the problem of finding a sampling that optimizes all importance functions as a *multi-objective optimization* problem. To solve this problem during an interactive exploration, we propose a selection algorithm that chooses a temporal sampling from a set of approximated optimal trade-off solutions (see Section 6.4). To compute these trade-off solutions, we compare two stochastic algorithms—a simulated annealing and an evolutionary algorithm for multi-objective optimization problems. The result of the presented technique is a sampling for a given temporal resolution which is an (approximated) optimal trade-off between all specified importance functions. Finally, we evaluate our method for three different real-world use cases, which exhibit different temporal characteristics and therefore require different temporal importance functions (see Section 6.5).

We do not propose a new visualization technique, but a technique to select data as input for other visualization algorithms during the analysis process. As we do not restrict ourselves to specific visualization algorithms, the resulting temporal subsamplings can be used as input data for all visualization algorithms operating on independent discrete data. Therefore, one major benefit of the proposed technique is that it can be integrated into existing visualization toolkits supporting time-varying data.

To summarize, the contributions of this chapter are:

- We propose a temporal importance model which integrates multiple notions of importance, in particular user knowledge and known visualization techniques.

- Given a desired temporal resolution, we introduce a technique that computes a non-uniform sampling of discrete time-varying data that approximates an optimal solution for all given notions of importance.

6.2. Temporal Importance

Scientific simulation data often comes in the form of discrete data defined at discrete time instants of the simulated process. As stated in Section 3.3.2, we assume that simulation data D consists of an ordered set $D = \{d_0, \ldots, d_{n-1}\}$ of discrete time steps. This set forms the input for visualization computations. In this chapter, we ignore the structure and size of the data contained in a time step d_i.

We define a *temporal sampling* of D with *temporal resolution* k to be a set P of discrete data $P = \{d_{i_0}, \ldots, d_{i_{k-1}}\}$. In our time model, this sampling is realized by an appropriate time index frame of size k, which maps k time indices to the selected k time steps within the complete $n-1$ data items. That is, to exchange the temporal sampling only the re-direction of time indices to time steps has to be changed. The desired size of a temporal sampling mainly depends on the availability of limited resources (e.g., memory) and acceptable response and animation duration times. Let Π_k be the set of all samplings for a temporal resolution k. The maximum temporal resolution has a single sampling $P_n = \{d_0, \ldots, d_{n-1}\}$ comprising all available discrete data items, that is $\Pi_n = \{P_n\}$. We define the minimum temporal resolution to be $k=1$, as at least one data item must be shown. Hence, it is obvious that $|\Pi_1| = n$. In general, the size of Π_k is $|\Pi_k| = \binom{n}{k}$. For reasonable values of k and n, finding the best sampling from this problem dimension is a hard task.

In order to compute such a "best" sampling, we first define the term importance to rank possible temporal samplings. As we deal with importance on a set of discrete time instants only, we introduce the term *temporal importance* to distance ourselves from work which deals with both importance in the temporal and spatial domain [19, 100, 101].

More formally, a temporal importance function $I(P) : \Pi_{|P|} \to \mathbb{R}$ maps an importance value to each temporal sampling. This importance value is used as a measure how well a temporal sampling fulfills some notion of importance. An example for importance functions are *accumulated importance functions* which are defined by a sum over the importance values for each discrete time step, i.e., $I(P) = \sum_{j=0}^{k-1} I(\{d_{i_j}\})$ for $P = \{d_{i_0}, \ldots, d_{i_{k-1}}\}$. This property does not hold for every importance function, e.g., importance by joint entropy [101] (see Section 6.3.3).

However, defining temporal importance is not trivial. Different scientists have different interests in their data, different parts of the data may exhibit more or less information, and the choice of data subsets can influence the efficiency of the visualization system. Therefore, we propose to classify the term temporal importance into three categories:

Interest This class contains all importance functions directly specified by the domain scientist who is analyzing the data. This includes interest derived from task-specific questions as well as domain knowledge or experience. Typically, interest is formulated in an imprecise way, e.g., by selecting time intervals, attribute value ranges [5], spatial regions [19], temporal patterns [44] or combinations thereof. Interest may change during the analysis session and is possibly frequently adapted by the user.

Information Time-varying data contains different kinds of information. This data can be automatically searched for regularity, irregularity or extrema, based both on information theory [60, 101] or domain-based theory [82, 85]. While these patterns are clearly describable, they need not exactly match the goal of the analysis process, but may give useful hints. Information-based importance functions do not change during the analysis session and are typically computed in a preprocessing step.

Interactivity Selecting certain time steps may be beneficial for the efficiency of the visualization computation. For example, single time steps already residing in memory are immediately available, required meta-structures are already built up or specific time steps require less memory than others. While this does not provide the user with more useful data, it can significantly improve the interactivity of the user's exploration. Interactivity information needs to be provided by the used visualization system and should be automatically collected.

These classes are not orthogonal, that is, a technique might belong to more than one class. For instance, a feature tracking technique extracts features in an automatic preprocess (information), but therefore requires an initial feature definition by the user (interest).

For a given set of importance functions, a temporal sampling should equally optimize all functions in this set. However, these three classes enable the user to prioritize certain notions of importance on a high level (e.g., "I'm more interested in an interactive work process" or "While precomputed information is helpful, I prioritize my specified interest."), which we will take advantage of in Section 6.4.5. In the next section, we introduce exemplary importance functions from all three classes.

6.3. Importance Functions

We devised a set of varying techniques to define importance functions, including examples from each of the three classes. This set is not meant to be complete and is open for extension by problem-specific importance functions. However, the proposed techniques are applicable to a wide range of domain problems. In addition, some of these importance functions should give examples, how

6.3. IMPORTANCE FUNCTIONS

existing techniques from the visualization community can be integrated into existing applications to influence a suitable sampling.

Following the taxonomy presented in Section 4.2, the specification of interest is an implicit way to select a non-uniform resolution. Because interest-based importance functions can be changed by the user during the analysis, we are going to briefly describe user interfaces when we address interest-based importance functions. Please refer to Section 4.3 to a discussion of advantages and disadvantages of certain 3D user interfaces.

6.3.1. Sketching Importance (*Interest*)

A very direct way for the domain scientist to express temporal interest is to directly draw a sketch of an importance curve. This technique is especially useful to express unclear or imprecise interest of the user, which cannot be formulated in a stricter way (e.g., "somewhere around this point in time"). In addition, it allows a fast expression of the user's mental representation of temporal importance. Figure 6.1 shows a remote 2D GUI (cf. Section 4.3.3) to sketch an importance curve. 3D GUIs are also possible, but lack the haptic feedback and accuracy of a remote mobile device.

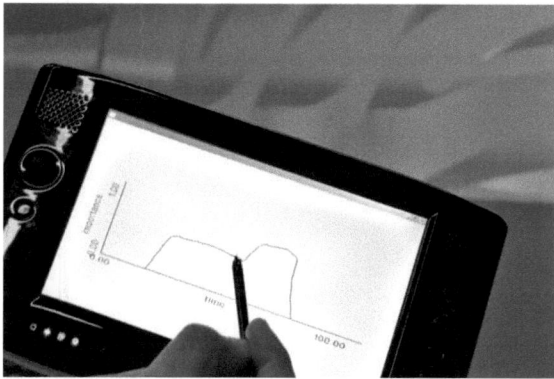

Figure 6.1.: The user directly sketches a temporal importance curve using a remote mobile device.

6.3.2. Description Language (*Interest*)

Inspired by the idea of Glatter et al. to describe temporal patterns by textual pattern matching [44], we propose to offer the user a textual interface to describe interesting temporal patterns and relationships. As we search for temporal patterns, only statistical data (average, standard deviation, histograms, or extrema attributes) within a time step or within a time-varying pre-extracted spatial region is regarded. The statistical data is collected in a preprocessing step. Thus, we are able to apply a more expressive language such as Linear Temporal Logic (LTL) including future and past operators. This language is mostly used in model checking; a formal definition of this logic was given by Lichtenstein et al. [71].

LTL resembles first-order logic extended by temporal operators (the unary operations "in the next time instant" X and "in the previous time instant" P, and the binary operations "until" U and "since" S). Other operators can be constructed from these, for instance $F\phi = trueU\phi$ means "finally" or "eventually". As in Glatter et al., multivariate queries are evaluated at discrete points in time. However, in LTL, queries are not restricted to range queries, but may consist of classical first-order logic propositions. For instance, the query for the pattern "after a (possibly empty) period where relative change was low (between -40% and 40%), the relative change rose above 40%" can be expressed by "[-.4-.4]*T[.4-max]?*" in the textual language of Glatter et al. or by "(r≥-0.4 ∧ r≤0.4) S (r≥0.4)" in LTL.

To specify LTL formulas, we provide the user with a textual scripting language to avoid the LTL notation which is unknown to most simulation scientists. As an example of this scripting language, the LTL formula avg(attribute) > 15.0 ∧ F(max(attribute) > 30.0) is denoted by

```
function example (data)
return  (data:GetFieldByName("attribute"):GetAverage() > 15.0)
        and EVENTUALLY (data:GetFieldByName("attribute"):GetMax()> 30.0))
end
```

Based on an LTL formula φ with future and past operators, we model an accumulated importance function as follows. For each time step d_i we compute the distance $D(d_i)$ to the next time step d_j with $d_j \models \varphi$, where $\models$ is the satisfaction of an LTL formula. These distances $D(d_i)$ are normalized to [0, 1]. Then, the importance value for this time step is $I(d_i) = e^{-\mu \cdot D(d_i)}$. This gives high importance values to time steps which satisfy the formula (i.e., the value one). Using the exponential function, neighboring time steps which may have led to the satisfaction are also included depending on the scaling factor μ.

To enter the LTL formula using the scripting language, a textual interface is required (cf. Section 4.3.2). If the structure of the formula is determined, but only the values of constants are changed, remote 2D or 3D GUIs can easily be used to modify these values.

6.3.3. Joint Entropy (*Information*)

Wang et al. proposed to select time step samples which maximize conditional entropy $H(d_{i_j}|d_{i_{j-1}})$ between neighboring time steps of a temporal sampling [101]. Entropy $H(X)$ is a measure of content of knowledge and therefore of the uncertainty of a random variable X. When regarding a certain attribute of a time step (e.g., the temperature) as a random variable, the conditional entropy $H(d_{i_j}|d_{i_{j-1}})$ determines the amount of uncertainty about the time step's data after the previous time step is known. We directly integrate the approach of Wang and colleagues as a temporal importance function. For a target resolution of size k, temporal importance of a sampling is given by the joint entropy of the collection of samples [27, Chapter 2]:

$$I(P) = H(d_{i_0}, \ldots, d_{i_{k-1}}) = \sum_{j=0}^{k-1} H(d_{i_j}|d_{i_{j-1}}, \ldots, d_{i_0}).$$

The idea behind this is to maximize the joint entropy of the chosen temporal sampling for a certain data attribute. Conditional entropy is computed by the mutual information between two time steps as described by Wang et al. [101]. For efficiency reasons, for each attribute mutual information $M(X;Y)$ between two time steps X and Y is computed within a restricted time window instead of computing mutual information between all time steps. We chose a time window of size three, which is the same value as used by Wang et al. That is, for time step d_i only mutual information values $M(d_i;Y)$ for $Y = d_{i-3}, \ldots, d_{i-1}, d_{i+1}, \ldots, d_{i+3}$ are computed. Then, conditional entropy $H(X|Y)$ equals $H(X|Y) = H(X) - M(X;Y)$, that is the uncertainty in X minus the mutual information between both time steps.

This importance function is distinguished from other typical importance functions, as temporal importance cannot be evaluated for a single discrete time step; here, it depends on the previously chosen sample time steps.

6.3.4. Features (*Interest + Information*)

The temporal evolution of user-defined features can be tracked [79]. Certain events or particular stages in the evolution of a feature can also be automatically detected (see, e.g., Reinders et al. [82]). These events of a user-specified feature represent potentially important points in time for the domain expert. Therefore, events can be used to construct an importance function over the set of discrete time steps. Not only the event, but also the temporal evolution leading to that event are of interest. Providing a higher resolution around the time instant of the event facilitates an analysis of the causes which have led to this event as well as what effects this event may have. Therefore, we model the importance induced by feature events as the union of Gaussian

CHAPTER 6. IMPORTANCE-BASED TEMPORAL SUBSAMPLING

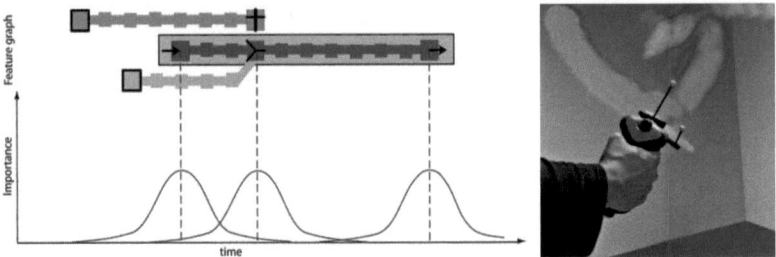

Figure 6.2.: Left: An importance function derived from a feature graph (using the notation of Reinders et al. [82]). The blue feature path is selected. For each event of this feature, a Gaussian curve is added to the importance function. The importance function equals the sum over all curves. Right: The user selects a feature in an immersive environment (courtesy of B. Hentschel [51]).

importance functions, with one Gaussian for each event. The time instant of an event is positioned at the mean value of the Gaussian curve. This results in a high importance value for each single event and strongly decreasing importance for the event's temporal vicinity (see Figure 6.2 left). Modifying the standard deviation influences the size of this vicinity.

The definition of features as well as the selection of events of interest require a user interface. We employ the interfaces for feature definition and feature analysis provided by the work of B. Hentschel [51] (see Figure 6.2 right). The same importance function can be used to resolve manually defined events, for instance time instants marked by a scientist using a time buoy (see Section 5.4).

6.3.5. Cached Data (*Interactivity*)

As most data sets with a high temporal resolution exceed the amount of available main memory, a visualization system has to constantly load discrete time step data from secondary storage during the exploration process. Caching of once used data can significantly shorten file I/O waiting times. However, if the selection of a new sampling ignores the currently cached data, this new selection can result in a large number of cache misses, which increase waiting times for the user. A simple importance function to avoid cache misses therefore assigns a positive value to time steps residing in cache, while non-cached data are assigned zero importance, resulting in a binary importance function:

$$I(d_i) = \begin{cases} 1 & \text{if } d_i \text{ cached,} \\ 0 & \text{else.} \end{cases}$$

In Chapter 7, we describe a parallel computation system that makes use of such a time step cache.

6.4. Subsampling Algorithm

Our main goal is to devise an algorithm which selects a (possibly) non-uniform sampling of a given temporal resolution as input for other visualization techniques. A prerequisite is a set of importance functions that has to be selected and defined by the user. The last section has shown several examples for importance functions.

Based on this specification of temporal importance, a subsampling algorithm should compute a sampling that maximizes all given importance functions. Besides computing a good solution, the algorithm has to meet two additional requirements:

1. The algorithm needs to return a result within acceptable waiting times to support an interactive exploration process [76]. That is, a new temporal sampling could be meaningful whenever the user restricts (or widens) the time interval currently under investigation (a target selection task, see Section 4.2) or focuses on other attributes of the data—and therefore changes his interest (an implicit resolution selection task, see Section 4.2). We suggest to compute a new sampling only on explicit request by the user, as this changes the data currently under investigation.

2. The algorithm should produce results without the need of fine-tuning or too many algorithm-specific parameters, as these parameters are not directly related to the user's task. This is required in the sense of Chen et al. for "...reducing the burden on users to acquire knowledge about complex visualization techniques" [24].

In order to fulfill these requirements, we propose an algorithm that first approximates the set of all optimal trade-offs for a given set of objectives within a predetermined time budget and then makes the final decision on the basis of these feasible trade-off solutions. The rationale behind this is, that we enable the user to articulate preference for one of the three importance classes in the final automatic decision step, but do not demand an a-priori input to steer the algorithm.

In order to define trade-offs between solutions, we introduce basic terms of multi-objective optimization (see Section 6.4.1). Following, we describe two different optimization algorithms that compute a set of optimal trade-offs: the Multi-Objective Simulated Annealing (MOSA) algorithm (see Section 6.4.2) and the extended Strength Pareto Evolutionary Algorithm (SPEA2, see Section

6.4.3). Finally, we select a single solution from this set (see Sections 6.4.5 and 6.4.6).

In the following sections, we will use the term *temporal sampling* and *solution* interchangeably, as a temporal sampling is a solution we are searching for.

6.4.1. Multi-Objective Optimization

Because the semantics of importance may highly vary with respect to the underlying analysis task, multiple importance functions can be combined to describe different aspects of what is important or interesting. Therefore, in this section, we formalize the search for a temporal sampling that optimizes multiple importance functions as a *multi-objective optimization problem* [31]. Multi-objective optimization problems are characterized by multiple goals towards which to optimize. As these objectives are usually competing, it is not always possible to locate a single solution which is better than all other solutions.

Assume we have r objectives $o_i(P), i = 0, \ldots, r-1$, which are temporal importance functions. Without loss of generality, we assume all objectives are to be maximized (minimization problems can be formulated as maximization problems by using inverse or negative values). The multi-objective optimization problem may be expressed as

$$\text{maximize } \bar{o}(P) \equiv (o_0(P), \ldots, o_{r-1}(P)).$$

In addition to a set of objectives, feasible solutions have to respect a set of constraints. A constraint c is given in terms of a function inequality $c(P) \leq g$ for some threshold value g. Equality constraints and strict inequality constraints are also possible.

In order to compare two possible solutions P and Q, we define the *dominance* relation [31]. Q is dominated by P, written $Q \prec P$, if P is no worse for all objectives than Q and better for at least one objective:

$$Q \prec P \Leftrightarrow \quad \forall i = 0, \ldots, r-1: \; o_i(P) \geq o_i(Q)$$
$$\wedge \exists j \; 0 \leq j \leq r-1: \; o_j(P) > o_j(Q).$$

A solution P is called *Pareto-optimal*, if no other feasible solution dominates P. The set of Pareto-optimal solutions is called the *Pareto-front*, which represents the optimal trade-offs between

6.4. SUBSAMPLING ALGORITHM

competing solutions. As a consequence, the Pareto-front consists of solutions that are mutually non-dominating.

A straightforward approach for multi-objective optimization is to optimize an aggregate function $f(P) = \sum_{i=0}^{r-1} w_i \cdot o_i(P)$, which weights each objective with a weight factor w_i. This approach has three major drawbacks. First, parts of the Pareto-front are inaccessible for fixed weights [29]. Second, this procedure results in a single solution only, without knowledge about alternative trade-offs. Third, the weights require numerical input by the user a-priori. However, the semantics of these weights are not intuitive, because they affect the resulting solution only indirectly.

To this end, we examine two dominance-based algorithms to approximate the Pareto-front in the following two sections: the Multi-Objective Simulated Annealing (MOSA) algorithm (see Section 6.4.2) and the extended Strength Pareto Evolutionary Algorithm (SPEA2, see Section 6.4.3). Both algorithms were chosen for the following four reasons. First, both are iterative algorithms. That is, they can be stopped after a given time budget and return a result (requirement 1). However, this result does not need to be optimal. Second, they avoid fixed weight factors, as they use the dominance relation to compare different objectives (requirement 2). Third, both require only a small number of input parameters which can often be determined by best practice heuristics (requirement 2). Fourth, both algorithms perform well on standard multi-objective optimization problems [93, 117].

6.4.2. Multi-Objective Simulated Annealing (MOSA)

Simulated annealing belongs to the class of stochastical algorithms. Essentially it is an iterative search for improvements using a Metropolis method [66]. Given a current solution, a possible solution for the next step is created by a slight random change to the current solution. New solutions that are an improvement are always accepted. To avoid premature termination in local optima, bad solutions are accepted with a certain probability, which is continuously lowered during the process according to a so called annealing schedule. This annealing process—which is inspired by the physical annealing of condensed matter—is steered by a Boltzman factor depending on a temperature parameter T.

To compute an approximated Pareto-front, we selected the multi-objective simulated annealing algorithm MOSA [93] proposed by Smith and colleagues. The main differences between MOSA and the standard simulated annealing algorithm are the used energy difference function and the applied perturbation function. In addition, as MOSA tries to approximate the Pareto-front, a set of mutually non-dominating solutions is maintained.

The dominance-based energy function proposed by Smith et al. [93] depends on the difference in the number of solutions dominated by two solutions. Given the set of (yet) mutually non-dominating solutions F, the current state x and a new state x', the sets $\tilde{F} := F \cup \{x\} \cup \{x'\}$, $\tilde{F}_x = \{y \in \tilde{F} \mid x \prec y\}$ and $\tilde{F}_{x'}$ (analogous) are computed. $\tilde{F}_x$ is the set of elements that dominate x. Now the energy difference between states x and x' is $\delta E(x, x') = \frac{1}{|\tilde{F}|}(\left|\tilde{F}_{x'}\right| - \left|\tilde{F}_x\right|)$.

In the perturbation step, a single random position of the temporal sampling is chosen and changed. While two main parameters are required to steer MOSA (i.e., the starting temperature and epoch size for equal temperatures), Smith et al. provide heuristic-based mechanisms to automatically adapt these parameters [93]. The starting solution is either the uniform sampling of the required size or the previous sampling. The latter is useful, if not all importance functions are changed at once, as a good starting solution results in faster convergence. A simplified version of MOSA is depicted in Algorithm 1.

Algorithm 1 MOSA

1: init feasible starting solution x
2: set of non-dominated solutions $F := \{\}$
3: initialize temperature T
4: **while** time not exceeded **do**
5:    $x' := \text{perturb}(x)$
6:    **if** $e^{\frac{-\delta E(x,x')}{T}} > \text{random\_number}(0,1)$ **then**
7:       x := x'
8:       **if** $x \not\prec z \;\forall z \in F$ **then**
9:          $F := \{z \in F \mid z \not\prec x\} \cup \text{x}$
10:       **end if**
11:    **end if**
12:    update T according to annealing schedule
13: **end while**

6.4.3. Multi-Objective Evolutionary Algorithm (SPEA2)

Evolutionary algorithms belong to a class of stochastical algorithms which try to simulate the process of natural evolution. Strongly simplified, a *population* P_0 of candidate solutions (called individuals) is iteratively modified via selection according to a fitness function and random variation of this selection.

Specifically, we chose the SPEA2 algorithm for multi-objective optimization [117]. Basic properties of SPEA2 are a domination-based fitness function and an external *archive* A with promising solutions to avoid loosing good solutions due to random effects. The archive A collects the best solutions that occured during the run of the algorithm.

6.4. SUBSAMPLING ALGORITHM

Algorithm 2 SPEA2
1: initialize starting population P_0
2: archive of promising solutions $A_0 := \{\}$
3: j:=0
4: **while** time not exceeded **do**
5:    assign fitness $F(x)$ $\forall x \in P_j \cup A_j$
6:    fill A_{j+1} according to low fitness values
7:    $P_{j+1} :=$ Variation (Selection (A_{j+1}))
8:    j:=j+1
9: **end while**

In each step j, the fitness function F first assigns each individual a strength value, which is the number of individuals it dominates, i.e., strength $S(x) = |\{z|z \in P_j \cup A_j \wedge z \prec x\}|$. Then, for each individual x fitness is computed by adding up the strength values of all individuals which dominate x, i.e.,

$$F(x) = \sum_{y \in P_j \cup A_j \wedge x \prec y} S(y).$$

Therefore, a high fitness value represents solutions which are dominated by many others, and a fitness value of zero indicates a non-dominated solution. The new archive is formed by filling it up with individuals with low fitness values.

Selection is done by binary tournament selection on the archive data only, that is the population does not participate in mating. For the variation step, mutation of samplings (i.e., changing a single entry) and recombination of two samplings (i.e., 1- and 2-point crossover recombination) are chosen with different probabilities. Necessary parameters for SPEA2 are the population and archive sizes, as well as probabilities for the single variations. The starting population is filled by variation of both the uniform sampling of the required size and the previous sampling. A simplified version of the SPEA2 main loop is depicted in Algorithm 2.

6.4.4. Constraints

In addition to the objective functions as input for the optimization algorithms, several constraints are also useful. As the optimization algorithms will select the more important time steps, without further constraints, this results in a sampling where time steps with high importance are covered very dense, while unimportant ones are not covered at all. To maintain a certain degree of coverage, a minimal and maximal distance between time steps should be enforced by means of constraints. However, as the exact value of these constraints is often not important, they can be determined by a heuristic (e.g., 10% of the number of time steps as the maximal distance and 0.1% as the

CHAPTER 6. IMPORTANCE-BASED TEMPORAL SUBSAMPLING

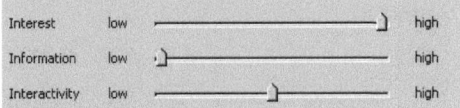

Figure 6.3.: 2D user interface to intuitively express preference for the categories interest, information and interactivity. The slider positions control weight factors for all importance functions that belong to the corresponding category.

minimal distance).

6.4.5. Selecting a Trade-off Solution

Both algorithms return a set of mutually non-dominating solutions, which approximates the Pareto-front. As only a single temporal sampling is required as solution, as a last step, we have to select a single result from this set of trade-offs. As stated earlier, leaving this decision a-posteriori is done to avoid the need for exact parametrization of the algorithms a-priori.

To select a trade-off solution, we utilize the Weighted Metrics Method [31]. The aim of the Weighted Metrics Method is to minimize the distance between the selected solution in objective space and the ideal objective vector z^*. This ideal objective vector $z^* = (z_0^*, \ldots, z_{r-1}^*)$ is defined by $z_i^* = \mathrm{argmax}\ o_i$, that is each component of this vector is the corresponding maximum i-th objective value. Hence, z^* defines which quality a solution can possibly reach. In general, this ideal objective vector does not belong to a feasible solution, as the objectives are conflicting. However, z^* serves as a reference point in objective space. Before selection, the objective space is normalized according to z^* in order to remove scaling effects of single objectives.

For a set of weights w_i with $w_i > 0$ for $i = 0, \ldots, r-1$ and $\sum_{i=0}^{r-1} w_i = 1$, and the ideal objective vector z^*, we select from the approximated Pareto-front Ψ a solution P using

$$\mathrm{argmin}_{P \in \Psi} \sqrt{\sum_{i=0}^{r-1} w_i \cdot (z_i^* - o_i(P))^2}$$

The weights can be used to emphasize single objectives. A fair trade-off between all objectives is selected by chosing all w_i to be equal. For unequal weights, objective scores with a higher weight have a stronger influence on the selection. The user can either choose the weights directly or set a weight for each of the three categories *interest, information* and *interactivity*. The latter influences all importance functions associated with the category. The benefit of this approach is

6.4. SUBSAMPLING ALGORITHM

a more abstract expression of preference. Figure 6.3 shows an exemplary 2D user interface to control these weights by manipulating preference between interest, information and interactivity. Here, weights are chosen on an abstract "low - high" scale.

Because the decision weights are chosen a-posteriori, they do not influence the algorithm directly. This is contrary to the a-priori weights utilized for a single aggregate function (see Section 6.4.1), where the numerical input strongly influences the resulting solution. In addition, for an already computed Pareto-front the user can interactively modify weight factors and receive immediate feedback of the selected solution without re-execution of the optimization algorithm.

6.4.6. Varying Resolution

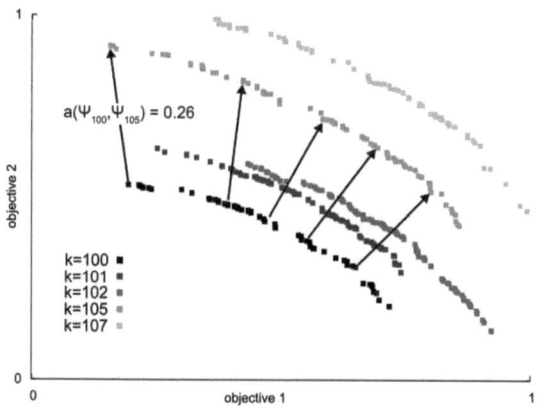

Figure 6.4.: An example for varying resolution. Depicted are approximated Pareto-fronts for different temporal resolutions in objective space, spanned by two normalized dimensionless objectives. In addition to the original resolution of k=100, approximated Pareto-fronts Ψ_k for k=101,102,105,107 were computed. For k=105, the average minimal distance $a(\Psi_{100}, \Psi_{105}) = 0.26$ is shown, which corresponds to a gain of $g(\Psi_{100}, \Psi_{105}) = 0.052$.

The target resolution size often is not a strict constraint. That is, to the domain scientist it is often not important, if for instance 102 instead of 100 discrete time steps are chosen. The exception is a memory constraint which must not be exceeded. However, a slight increase of resolution may result in a significant benefit.

In the case of the genetic algorithm, a first approach is to include a possible increase of resolution in the mutation step. However, individuals with higher resolution quickly dominate all other individuals, disposing all individuals with the orginally desired resolution. Therefore, increasing resolution needs to be evaluated separately from the optimization step. We propose the following approach: Whenever a sampling for a temporal resolution for size k is computed by the selection algorithm, samplings for resolutions of size $m > k$ are computed concurrently. The number of samplings that are computed concurrently depends on the parallel computing resources available. To decide if a higher resolution should be accepted instead of the desired resolution, we quantify the relative gain of a high resolution as follows. Let d be the distance between two samplings P, Q in objective space, that is

$$d(P, Q) = \|(o_0(P), \ldots, o_{r-1}(P))^T - (o_0(Q), \ldots, o_{r-1}(Q))^T\|_2.$$

To remove scaling effects of single objectives, this distance is measured in the normalized objective space. Given two approximated Pareto-fronts $\Psi \subseteq \Pi_k$ and $\Theta \subseteq \Pi_m$, the average minimal distance $a(\Psi, \Theta)$ between Ψ and Θ is

$$a(\Psi, \Theta) = \frac{1}{|\Psi|} \sum_{P \in \Psi} \mathrm{argmin}_{Q \in \Theta}(d(P, Q)).$$

For $k < m$, the relative gain from Ψ to Θ is given by the difference quotient

$$g(\Psi, \Theta) = \frac{a(\Psi, \Theta)}{m - k}.$$

That is, the relative gain correlates the distance in objective space between two fronts to their difference in resolution size. Now, a set of approximated Pareto-fronts is maintained—either computed in a preprocess or a set of previously computed resolutions during runtime— and the average gain $\bar{g}$ of this set is computed. To decide if an alternative front Θ for a higher resolution is beneficial compared to the original front Ψ, $g(\Psi, \Theta) > \bar{g}$ is evaluated. The fundamental idea of this approach is to accept a higher resolution only if the gained benefit is larger than the usually expected benefit from an increase in resolution.

An example for this procedure is illustrated in Figure 6.4. For a desired size of k=100, four alternatives with up to 7% more time steps are computed. An average relative gain $\bar{g} = 0.08$ is determined from a set of pre-computed Pareto-fronts from k=10 to k=800 (not shown here). This preprocess took approximately two minutes, because 20 Pareto-fronts were computed with a time budget of five seconds. The described gain of $k = 105$ is too low to justify a raise in resolution; the front for $k = 101$ provides a relatively high gain $g(\Psi_{100}, \Psi_{101}) = 0.16$ and is therefore an acceptable variation.

6.5. Results

We apply three use cases from different fields of research to evaluate the proposed method (see Section 6.5.1). In order to analyze the proposed algorithm, we varied the input parameters time budget (see Section 6.5.2), target resolution size (see Section 6.5.3) and choice of importance functions (see Section 6.5.4). For all three use cases, all other parameters remained the same. The presented quantitative results are dimensionless scores for the importance functions; an interpretation of these scores need not be given. An exception is the score for the cached data importance function, which is equal to the (average) number of cache hits scored by the chosen sampling.

The presented scores are averaged scores from 20 runs. As the used optimization algorithms are stochastic, scores of single runs can vary. However, from our experiments, the presented values capture the overall behavior of both stochastic algorithms. To obtain comparable results, variation was avoided and only the uniform sampling was used as a starting solution. Results were measured on a workstation equipped with an Intel Core 2 Quad processor at 2.83 GHz and 4 GB of main memory.

6.5.1. Use Cases

In order to evaluate the proposed method we present three use cases from different fields of research. For each use case, a selection of task-specific importance functions from the examples given in Section 6.3 was chosen. In addition, we show examples for optimized samplings achieved with our approach (for a given target subsampling size k).

Nasal Airflow

In this section we discuss as the simulation of the unsteady flow of nasal respiration (see Section C.1) a use case. The data set resolves a full respiration cycle, i.e., one inhalation and exhalation period, with a high temporal resolution. For the analysis, the 2nd out of 4 such cycles with a small overlap to the first and third cycle was chosen, resulting in 5000 discrete time steps and 132 GB of raw data.

For this visualization, we integrated three importance functions:

- The transitions between inhalation and exhalation were identified to be unsteady, while the periods in between can be considered quasi-steady [57]. Therefore, time steps with an average

CHAPTER 6. IMPORTANCE-BASED TEMPORAL SUBSAMPLING

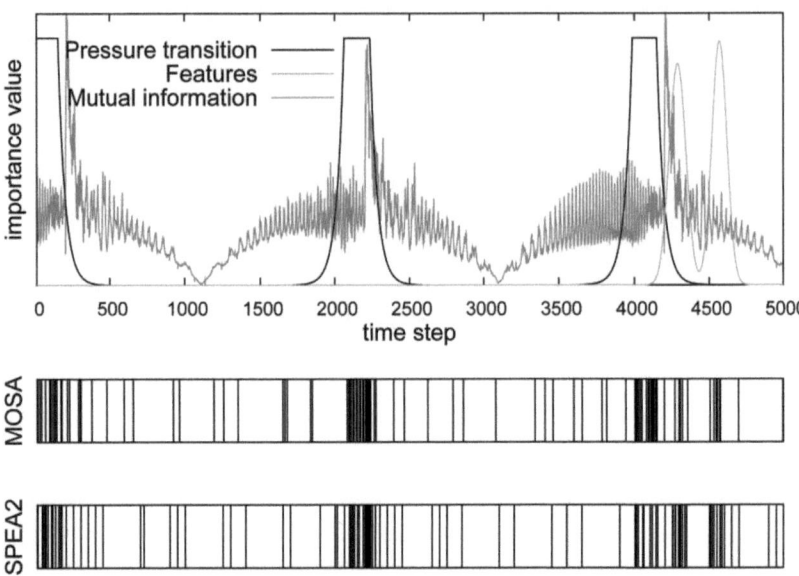

Figure 6.5.: Importance functions and selected temporal samplings for the nasal airflow data set.

pressure value around $\bar{p} = 0.65$ (dimensionless) showing this transition are interesting. This fact is reflected by a formula $\varphi = p > 0.95 \cdot \bar{p} \wedge p < 1.05 \cdot \bar{p}$, where p is the static pressure (see Section 6.3.2).

- Interesting features in the data set are vortex structures that are defined by regions of negative λ_2 [62]. These features were extracted and tracked in a preprocess. In the analysis process, two vortices in the left part of the lower and upper turbinate were selected. Events detected in these two features define a second importance function (see Section 6.3.4). For each feature, the existing birth and death events are close to one another and therefore add up to a single peak in the importance function.

- In a preprocess, mutual information over static pressure was computed. Using the method by Wang et al. [101], the third importance function is integrated to favor temporal samplings with a high joint entropy. Figure 6.5 depicts mutual information values for a time window of three (see Section 6.3.3).

A maximum distance between time steps of 300 and a minimum distance of 3 were used as constraints. The importance functions along the time domain as well as exemplary temporal samplings ($k = 100$) are shown in Figure 6.5.

Geothermal Reservoir Simulation

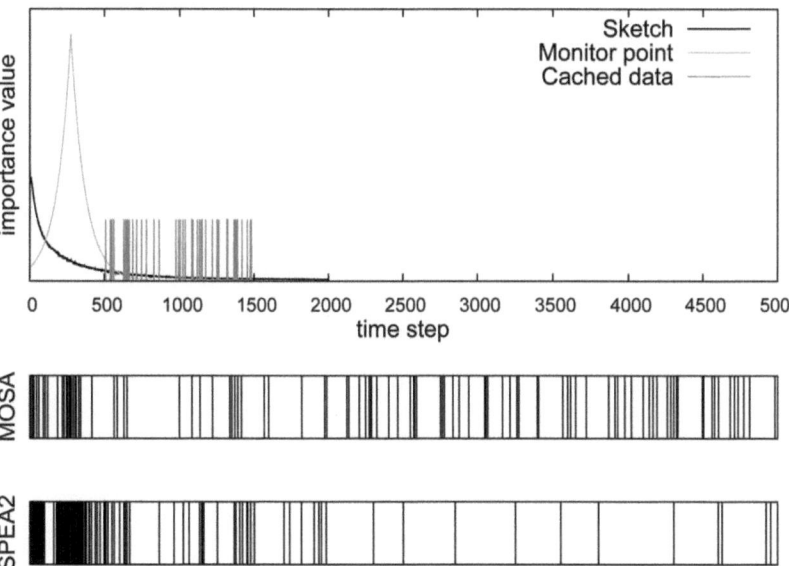

Figure 6.6.: Importance functions and selected temporal samplings for the geothermal data set.

In this geothermal reservoir simulation, a planned deep geothermal installation is forecasted using a horizon of 100 years with a nearly weekly time resolution, which results in 5000 time steps (see Section C.2). For this visualization, we integrated three importance functions. The first two are based on discussions with the simulation scientists:

- The user directly sketches an importance curve. The domain scientist knew from experience, that the system evolves according to the function drawn in Figure 6.6 (see Section 6.3.1).

- For a given monitor point in the simulation—that is, a spatial point within the reservoir area—, the domain scientists are interested in time steps where the temperature at this monitor point starts decreasing faster, after an initially slow decrease, as the cold water front from the injection well passes the monitor point. This is formulated by an LTL formula $\psi = (\Delta T_{\text{monitor}} < T_1) \wedge X(\Delta T_{\text{monitor}} > T_2)$, where T is temperature (see Section 6.3.2), T_1 is the threshold for slow decrease, and T_2 is the threshold for fast decrease. Using this formula, the time steps at which the cold water from the injection hole has reached the monitor point are assigned higher importance.

- To enable an interactive analysis of the data, cached results should be re-used if possible

CHAPTER 6. IMPORTANCE-BASED TEMPORAL SUBSAMPLING

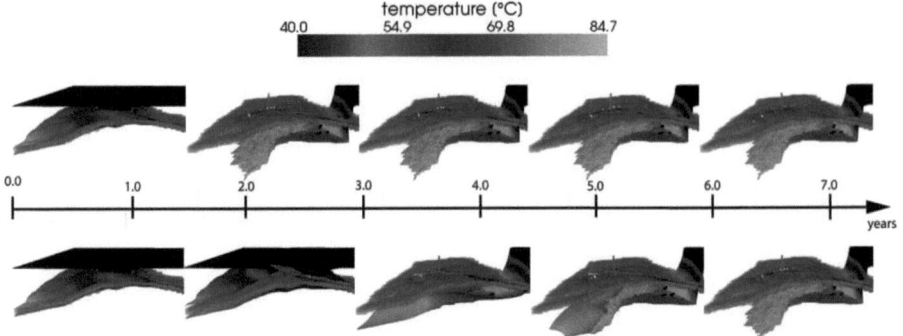

Figure 6.7.: The first five time steps of a uniform (top) and a non-uniform sampling (bottom) based on the user's sketch for the first seven years of the geothermal data set. Depicted is an isosurface of hydraulic head (a measure of water pressure differences), colored by temperature. Red dashes on the timeline indicate samples. While the depicted contour does not change significantly from the second time step of the uniform sampling onwards, the non-uniform sampling resolves the development of the contour more accurately (non-uniform samples after the fifth are not shown here).

whenever a new sampling is computed. Therefore, the binary cached data importance function is integrated (see Section 6.3.5). The cache was filled with 50 random time steps in the range from time step 500 to 1500.

A maximum distance between time steps of 500 and a minimum distance of 5 were used as constraints. The importance functions along the time domain as well as exemplary temporal samplings ($k = 100$) are shown in Figure 6.6. To show the benefit of a non-uniform sampling, Figure 6.7 compares the results obtained by a non-uniform sampling to the uniform sampling.

Ventricular Assist Device

The last use case is the visualization of the MicroMed DeBakey Ventricular Assist Device® (see Section C.3). The used visualization shows 10,000 discrete time steps for 50 rotations of the rotating impeller.

For this visualization, we integrated three importance functions that are based on discussions with the simulation scientists:

- The user directly sketches an importance curve. As high hemolysis is assumed to occur due to rotary motion, the user manually marks the temporal residence interval of the particle

6.5. RESULTS

traces in the rotating geometry element (see Section 6.3.1).

- Interesting parts in the time-varying particle traces are characterized by a high rate of hemolysis. This function is given by a formula $\varphi = \Delta H > c$, where ΔH is the rate of hemolysis and c a user-chosen threshold (see Section 6.3.2). While this expression does not contain any temporal attributes, it is still a valid LTL formula.

- To correlate a possible effect for these regions of high hemolysis, a temporal pattern describing time steps with high shear stress after which at later time (i.e., we apply the "eventually" LTL-operator F) a high hemolysis rate follows is of interest. This is formulated by an LTL formula $\psi = (\sigma > c_1) \wedge F(\Delta H > c_2)$, where σ is shear stress and c_1, c_2 are some user-chosen thresholds (see Section 6.3.2).

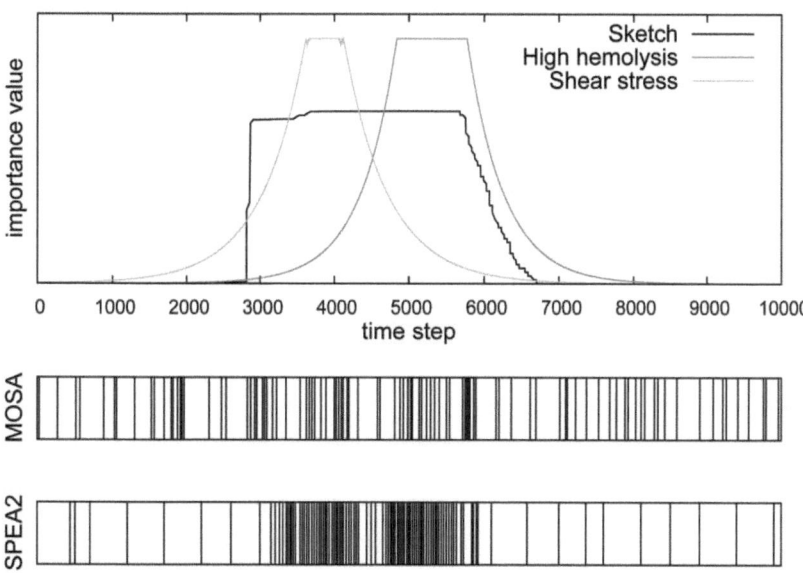

Figure 6.8.: Importance functions and selected temporal samplings for the blood pump data set.

A maximum distance between time steps of 500 and a minimum distance of 20 were used as constraints. The importance functions along the time domain as well as exemplary temporal samplings ($k = 100$) are shown in Figure 6.8.

6.5.2. Time budget t

Both optimization algorithms can be stopped after an arbitrary runtime. While this ensures a result after a certain waiting time, the retrieved result is possibly an inferior solution. To assess the effect of the given time budget on quality, we evaluated the distance of the generated set of solutions Ψ_t after a predefined runtime t to an assumed global optimal solution Ψ^* in objective space.

As the optimal solutions for the three use cases are not known, we generated for each use case an approximated Pareto-front Ψ^* that we assume to be near the global optimum solution. Based on the assumption that the utilized optimization algorithms converge after a certain runtime towards the optimal solution, we used the following two-step algorithm to compute Ψ^*: First, we repeatedly executed both optimization algorithms for 5 minutes and collected the resulting sets of solutions. Second, we extracted all mutually non-dominating solutions from the union of these sets and inserted them into a single set Ψ^*. We assume this set Ψ^* to be a good approximation of the global Pareto-front.

In order to analyze the effect of the given time budget, both optimization algorithms were executed for different runtimes from 100 ms to 5 seconds (i.e., 100 ms, 500 ms, 1 s, 2.5 s, 5 s). These runtimes were selected as they correspond to different categories of acceptable HCI response times as defined by Miller [76]. For each single runtime t and each optimization algorithm, we computed 50 approximated Pareto-fronts and merged these sets again into a single set Ψ_t of mutually non-dominating solutions. This was done in order to combine results from multiple repetitions.

The distance of Ψ_t for a specific runtime to the assumed optimal solution Ψ^* was measured using the average minimal distance $a(\Psi_t, \Psi^*)$. That is, a distance near to zero corresponds to a near optimal solution set, while a larger distance corresponds to a less optimal solution set. All measurements were generated for a fixed target subsampling of size $k = 100$.

Table 6.1 shows the measured distances for all three use cases. The distance values are normalized by the distance of the uniform solution and therefore represent the relative improvement from the starting solution (value 1.0) to the optimal solution (value 0.0). Starting with the uniform subsampling as a starting solution, both algorithms provide improved results even after a short response time of 100 ms. However, while such an interactive response time would be desirable, the distance to the assumed optimal solution Ψ^* is still large (i.e., ≥ 0.79).

Differences in convergence towards Ψ^* can be observed both regarding the optimization algorithm (i.e., MOSA or SPEA2) as well as the use case. For the nasal airflow data set, both algorithms converge fast to a good solution set, although MOSA does not improve much after a runtime

6.5. RESULTS

Use case	Algorithm	0.1 s	0.5 s	1 s	2.5 s	5 s
Nasal airflow	uniform	1.0	1.0	1.0	1.0	1.0
	MOSA	0.88	0.5	0.24	0.19	0.19
	SPEA2	0.79	0.31	0.22	0.07	0.03
Geothermal reservoir	uniform	1.0	1.0	1.0	1.0	1.0
	MOSA	0.96	0.81	0.65	0.64	0.66
	SPEA2	0.94	0.7	0.56	0.31	0.16
Ventricular assist device	uniform	1.0	1.0	1.0	1.0	1.0
	MOSA	0.97	0.72	0.61	0.58	0.46
	SPEA2	0.9	0.53	0.38	0.12	0.05

Table 6.1.: Average minimal distance of the resulting solution sets to an assumed Pareto-front for varying time budgets. The shown distance values are normalized to the distance of the uniform solution. Values closer to zero represent solution sets closer to the assumed global optimum Ψ^*.

of 2.5 s. For the geothermal reservoir simulation, the computed solutions improve slower than for the nasal airflow data set. After a runtime of 1 s, the MOSA optimization does not improve significantly and in average even produces worse results after 5 seconds than after 2.5 seconds. For the ventricular assist device, SPEA2 comes close to Ψ^* after 5 seconds, while MOSA converges much slower and covers only half the distance from the starting solution to the optimum solution front. The effect of the slower convergence of MOSA compared to SPEA2 is also apparent in the exemplary resolutions shown in Figures 6.5, 6.6 and 6.8. These exemplary results computed with a time budget of 2.5 s show that when using MOSA, unimportant regions are still sampled by multiple single time steps.

In summary, SPEA2 converges faster than MOSA to towards Ψ^*. For the selected target resolution size $k = 100$, good results are achieved within a time budget of 5 seconds. The influence of the target resolution size on the result quality is analyzed in the next section.

6.5.3. Subsampling Size k

The size k of a temporal resolution is chosen by the user based on available memory or computing resources. To analyze the effect of k on the quality of the computed samplings, we computed temporal resolutions using our selection algorithm for a fixed time budget $t = 2$ s and equal weights w_i for the selection step. We chose a time budget that is consistent with an acceptable waiting time for the user [76], which corresponds to the typical interactive usage scenario (see Section 6.4). Measurements were carried out for four different resolution sizes $k = 50, 100, 250, 500$. The reported scores are averages from 20 runs.

Figure 6.9 shows the results of these measurements for all three use cases. From these results,

CHAPTER 6. IMPORTANCE-BASED TEMPORAL SUBSAMPLING

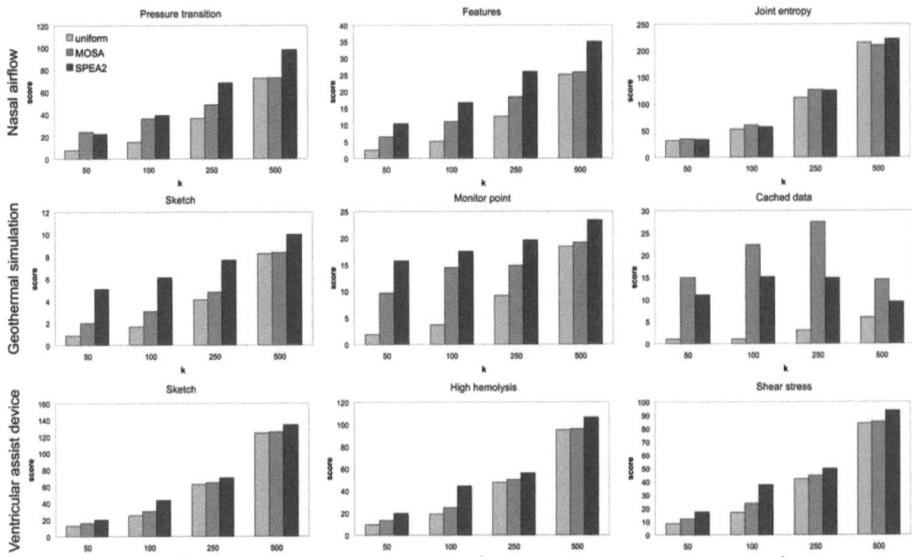

Figure 6.9.: Scores for selected solutions of the importance functions (columns) of all three use cases (rows) using a uniform subsampling, MOSA, and SPEA2 for varying subsampling sizes k. The legend is shown in the first chart.

the following general observation can be made. First, both MOSA and SPEA2 outperform the uniform subsampling. Using the proposed optimization approach, similar or even higher scores can be achieved with significantly less time steps. As an example, when regarding the nasal airflow's pressure transition importance function, SPEA2 scores a value of 38.85 with $k = 100$, while the uniform resolution needs 250 time steps to score a value of 36.65.

Second, for accumulated importance functions the SPEA2 optimization outperforms the MOSA optimization scores. Only for the non-accumulated importance functions—i.e., the cached data importance function and the joint entropy function—MOSA mostly outperforms SPEA2. This effect is marginal for the joint entropy function, but clearly visible in the cached data function. This observation is explained by the locality of changes made by both algorithms: MOSA applies only local changes (i.e., one time step at a time), while SPEA2 uses in addition a crossover-recombination that mixes two existing solutions. In particular for the binary cached data importance function, finding single cached time steps is only possible with local changes.

Third, for a growing resolution size k the relative improvement to the uniform solution decreases significantly. That is, the smaller the target size, the higher the improvement to the starting solution after the fixed time budget of two seconds. In particular for the non-accumulated importance functions a relatively low performance for $k = 500$ can be observed. The latter effect originates

6.5. RESULTS

from the higher number of decision variables to be considered in the optimization algorithms, as each time step of the target resolution represents a decision variable. To quantify this effect, we measured the time per iteration of the optimization algorithms. For the SPEA2 algorithm this time increases for $k = 100$ from 8 ms (MOSA 0.04 ms) to 16 ms (MOSA 0.11 ms) for $k = 500$ (measured using the geothermal reservoir use case). That is, due to the larger number of decision variables, the time required for each iteration increases, which for a fixed time budget results in lesser numbers of optimization iterations. Consequently, within the available time budget the computed solutions are improved compared to the starting solution, but did not converge long enough towards the optimum solution. Table 6.2 lists the average minimal distances of the computed solutions for $k = 500$ after 5 and 10 seconds to the assumed optimal Pareto-front Ψ^* for this resolution. Even after 5 seconds, the normalized distances to the optimal front are quite high, which indicates that additional runtime is required to converge towards Ψ^*. Distances using the MOSA algorithm are even worse, because MOSA is restricted to changing one decision variable at a time only. This is a significant disadvantage for temporal resolutions that exhibit a high number of decision variables.

Use case	Algorithm	5 s	10 s
Nasal airflow	uniform	1.0	1.0
	MOSA	0.82	0.82
	SPEA2	0.21	0.09
Geothermal simulation	uniform	1.0	1.0
	MOSA	0.71	0.64
	SPEA2	0.48	0.24
Ventricular assist device	uniform	1.0	1.0
	MOSA	0.83	0.8
	SPEA2	0.57	0.36

Table 6.2.: Average minimal distance of the resulting solution sets to an assumed Pareto-optimal front for $k = 500$ and time budgets of 5 and 10 seconds. The shown distance values are normalized to the distance of the uniform solution. Values closer to zero represent solution sets closer to the assumed global optimum Ψ^*.

6.5.4. Combination of Importance Functions

To analyze the influence of the choice from a given set of objectives, we selected the nasal airflow data set. The importance functions defined in this use case are quite disjunct, that is they highlight different parts of the time-varying data (cp. Figure 6.5). Figure 6.10 shows the obtained scores for all three importance functions when the algorithms optimized only a subset of the available objectives. Measurements were conducted for a subsampling size $k = 100$, a time budget $t = 2$ s, and equal weights w_i for the selection step. The reported scores are averages from 20 runs.

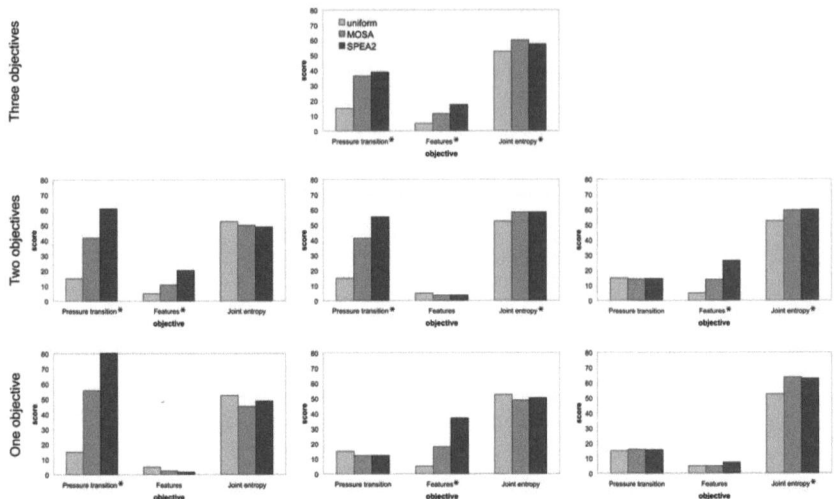

Figure 6.10.: Scores for all three importance functions of the nasal airflow dataset using a uniform subsampling, MOSA, and SPEA2. Only the importance functions that are marked by an asterik * were optimized by the optimization algorithms. All other values represented unoptimized scores. The legend is shown in the first chart.

The results show that an optimization of all three importance functions yields as expected score improvements for all three objectives. When optimizing only a subset, unoptimized importance functions achieve similar or even lower scores compared to the uniform subsampling. At the same time, discarding one or two objectives can result in higher scores for the remaining importance functions (i.e., the importance functions that are optimized), because solutions that exhibit low scores in the discarded objectives are not dominated any more. An example in Figure 6.10 is the pressure transition importance function. When optimized together with the vortex features objective or the joint entropy objective, SPEA2 scores pressure transition values of 60.86 or 55.24, respectively. When optimized as a single objective, SPEA2 yields a score of 80.23.

Results for the other two use cases show the same tendency, but the scores do not differ as noticable as using the nasal airflow data set.

6.5.5. Discussion

The presented results show that the proposed approach—utilizing both MOSA and SPEA2—generates samplings which adapt better to multiple objectives, i.e., it achieves higher scores compared to the uniform subsampling. Expressed differently, similar scores can be achieved by select-

6.5. RESULTS

ing a smaller number of time steps compared to a uniform subsampling. Uniform sampling can by chance be a good choice for single objectives—for instance joint entropy in cyclic phenomena, as seen in the nasal airflow use case. However, in the majority of cases the uniform subsampling does not adequately resolve important regions.

Both optimization algorithms adapt well even to non-accumulated or binary importance functions. However, MOSA seems to have advantages for these special importance functions and achieves better results than SPEA2. The reason is that MOSA manipulates the current sampling only locally (i.e., one time step at a time), while SPEA2 in addition uses crossover-recombination that mixes two samplings. For non-accumulated importance functions, using only local optimization is beneficial. Another advantage of the MOSA algorithm is, that it has less parameters to tune than SPEA2, where population sizes and variation probabilities need to be decided.

For accumulated importance functions, SPEA2 mostly reaches higher scores and converges faster to a good solution. This is due to the larger variation in genetic algorithms compared to the local changes in simulated annealing. We varied the existing parameters of our SPEA2 implementation— i.e., population sizes and variation probabilities—but did not find a significant effect on the resulting resolutions' quality (results not shown here). Therefore we argue that the higher number of parameters for SPEA2 compared to MOSA is no crucial disadvantage. On account of the better overall results and faster convergence, we recommend to use SPEA2 for optimization of importance functions.

However, we identified several limitations to the presented approach. First, due to the stochastic nature of the optimization algorithms, good results are not guaranteed within a bounded runtime. Inferior solutions are possible. Nevertheless, the results show that even these inferior scores typically outperform the uniform solution. Second, the runtimes of the optimization algorithms depend on the complexity of the importance functions. If the user integrates a time-consuming importance function, this likely leads to the computation of inferior results given a limited time budget. Therefore, complex importance functions should be pre-computed if possible (e.g., as done with the conditional entropy function).

Third, for a high target resolution size k result quality decreases significantly within interactive response times. Even for a target resolution of size $k = 500$ that corresponds to 10% of the nasal airflow's or geothermal reservoir's entire resolution or only 5% of the blood pump's, computation times beyond 5 seconds are required for good results. As a consequence, the computation of large temporal resolutions is not possible using our approach with an immediate response time, but requires computation times of ten's of seconds. However, we argue that while an interactive response time is desirable, a non-interactive response time needs not to be critical, depending on the frequency of *resolution selection* tasks (cf. Section 4.2) in the analysis process. During the exploratory analysis phase, temporal resolution is changed more frequently. Therefore we advise to explore using a lower temporal resolution (i.e., from 50 up to 250 time steps). During the search phase, hints for phenomena of interest are already found. We therefore assume a less frequent changing of temporal resolution, in particular interest-based importance functions. In particular when the user can proceed with other tasks (e.g., modifying the shown visualizations in the focus phase) while a temporal resolution is computed, a response time of above 15 seconds is acceptable [76]. In the focus phase, the investigated temporal interval is restricted to the focused phenomenon. Here, a temporal resolution of 50 to 250 time steps is often fully sufficient, as only a fraction of the entire temporal data is shown. In summary, our approach can be applied in all three phases and we expect severe restrictions in the search phase only. Still, a selection algorithm that provides immediate response times with high-quality solutions is desirable and remains a topic for future work.

Fourth, our approach is not scalable. Algorithm runtime depends on the target resolution k and not on the available temporal resolution. That is, the shown results and limitations for fixed target resolutions will be comparable to results that we can achieve when the large time-varying data consists of 10^5 or 10^6 time steps. However, for such large data, the relative resolution of the target sampling decreases significantly, and computing a resolution comprising 10% of the time steps—which corresponds to a target resolution $k = 10^4$ or $k = 10^5$—will not be feasible within acceptable response times. The significance of this drawback depends on the phenomenon under investigation. If the phenomenon covers the entire temporal range and a very fine temporal resolution is necessary to accurately depict the phenomenon, the temporal resolution our approach computes within short response times will not be sufficient. On the other hand, if the phenomenon is either temporally short or visible using a coarser resolution, the proposed approach is still applicable for very large time-varying data.

Fifth, it remains an open problem how to choose importance functions to find a desired phenomena. The selection algorithm optimizes only the specified objectives. Whether a phenomenon is resolved by the resulting temporal resolution in a suffient way depends on the user's choice and parametrization of the used importance functions. In addition, our algorithm just selects discrete time steps. Describing and finding the investigated phenomenon within these time steps by a suitable visualization algorithm is still the main task of the scientist analyzing data. Therefore, it is hard to evaluate how much our technique, in general, supports the user in finding phenomena of interest.

6.6. Summary

In this chapter, we have proposed a technique to select a suitable temporal sampling for a set of different importance functions. This selection algorithm can be used to execute *resolution selection* tasks by an implicit definition of importance (see Section 4.2). By supporting different notions of importance, a combination of user interest, domain knowledge, automatic information extraction and interactivity requirements can be integrated into this process. We have shown examples for possible importance functions from these domains, and used them in combination in three use cases.

To compute a temporal sampling, we have proposed a selection algorithm that tries to find an optimal trade-off between all given importance functions. We have evaluated and have compared two stochastical algorithms to compute the set of approximated optimal trade-off solutions, MOSA and SPEA2. The manipulation of decision weights—even in an abstract way—enables the user to select solutions along the computed Pareto-front that suits his preferences.

Our technique is applicable in an interactive exploration process and tries to reduce the amount of necessary parameters. In addition, it can easily be integrated in existing visualizations that operate on independent discrete time steps. The limitations of our approach have been discussed and significantly depend on the user's analysis behavior as well as the phenomenon under investigation. The use cases have shown, that an adapted temporal sampling is superior to a uniform sampling, but particularly so when multiple objectives need to be optimized. By using our selection algorithm, the necessary computational load to compute visualizations can be significantly decreased, while remaining important temporal regions of the time-varying data.

CHAPTER 7

A PARALLEL SYSTEM FOR COMPUTATION OF TIME-VARYING VISUALIZATIONS

7.1. Introduction

The computational problem described in Chapter 1 states that the visualization of large time-varying data causes a huge computational load, because visualization data has to be computed for each single time step. The subsampling algorithm proposed in the previous chapter helps to lessen this computational load by reducing the number of time steps for which visualization computations have to be executed. However, to achieve a good subsampling, a significant number of time steps is still required. Even if the phenomenon of interest can be resolved at 5% or 10% of the data set's temporal resolution, for large time-varying data this still amounts to hundreds of time steps.

To compute time-independent visualizations on this reduced resolution within acceptable waiting times, the remaining computational load has to be dealt with. To this end, this chapter describes a parallel system which facilitates efficient computation of time-independent visualizations. We exploit the scalability enabled by parallel computing as an effective countermeasure against the increasing temporal resolution of simulation data. In the following, we are going to use the term *visualization* to denote any kind of visualization primitive or geometric data that are produced during the visualization process and are used as input for rendering. Thus, we neglect the rendering part of visualization, which is not handled by the parallel system described here. However, this restriction enables us to use the brief term "compute a visualization" to describe the computational part of visualization (i.e., data loading, filtering, and mapping).

In order to parallelize the visualization of large time-varying data, the computation has to be decomposed into a collection of subtasks. Two fundamental approaches for this decomposition exist: decomposition of the set of time steps into subtasks or decomposition of each single time step. The latter approach is appropriate if the computation can be sped up to an interactive runtime, that is, parameter changes by the user update the shown visualization within 100 ms [18] or faster. However, the efficient decomposition of a set of discrete time steps into subtasks requires knowledge about the specific visualization algorithm, because the individual subtask's results have to be combined to a valid overall result for the discrete time step data. Because our goal is to compute general, time-independent visualizations, this approach is not applicable. The former approach—i.e., decomposition of the set of time steps into subtasks—is applicable for general time-independent visualizations as the subtasks' results are independently combined in the animation. For this reason, we regard single time steps as subtasks of our parallelization. It has to be noted though that parallel computation of a single time step in addition to the time-independent decomposition—for instance using thread-level parallelization—can significantly improve the overall performance and should therefore not be altogether ignored. Examples for such hybrid parallelizations are given in previous work [42, 53, 54, 110].

This chapter is structured as follows. First, we give an overview of the Viracocha parallelization system [40] that provides the basic software framework (see Section 7.2). Second, we describe in detail the enhancements we integrated into Viracocha that in particular target time-independent visualizations (see Section 7.3). One of these enhancements is the possibility to vary the scheduling algorithm that distributes time steps to processes. On this basis, the third part—Section 7.4— discusses performance-improving scheduling strategies as well as new scheduling strategies that incorporate the task analysis elaborated in Section 4.2.

7.2. Viracocha Architecture

The Viracocha parallelization framework [40] was developed in order to speed-up computational fluid dynamics (CFD) post-processing, in particular for immersive visualization within virtual environments. It follows the idea of the Distributed Virtual Windtunnel [17] to decouple rendering and computation. The reason for this is, that high rendering performance and high computing performance—combined with large amounts of memory—was (and typically still is) provided by different kinds of machines. Viracocha is employed in a client-server paradigm, which is the dominating paradigm for parallel visualization tools (see Section 2.5). The client part is provided by the ViSTA FlowLib library [87]. ViSTA FlowLib contains methods and data structures for

7.2. VIRACOCHA ARCHITECTURE

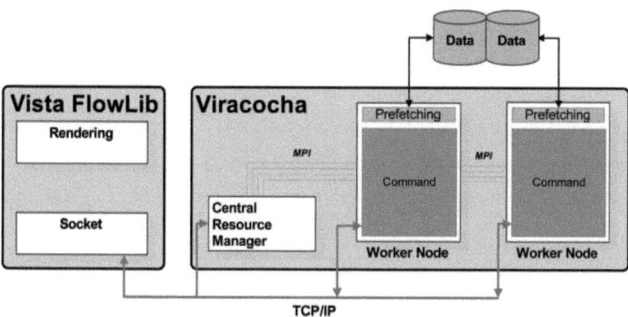

Figure 7.1.: Overview of the Viracocha architecture as described by Gerndt in 2006 [39].

the analysis of time-varying scientific data in virtual environments. The FlowLib client's main purposes are user interaction (e.g., time navigation) and rendering of visualization data.

An extensive description of the Viracocha system can be found in the PhD thesis of A. Gerndt [39]. Here, we are going to briefly outline the existing Viracocha system, which builds the technical starting point of this chapter. Important system-related terms are summarized in Appendix A.

Figure 7.1 depicts an overview of the Viracocha architecture. A ViSTA FlowLib application acts as a client. Using a high-level socket component (OSI *application layer*), the client application sends visualization *requests* to Viracocha that acts as a computing server. Each request typically comprises the description and parametrization of an algorithm as well as the description of the algorithm's input data. TCP/IP is employed as low-level network protocol (OSI *transport* and *network layers*). The requests are received by the *central resource manager* or *scheduler* process. This scheduler is a dedicated management process that communicates using the Message Passing Interface (MPI) with a group of computing or *worker* processes. All requests are stored by the scheduler until all computing processes specified by the client's request are available. When enough computing processes are idle, the scheduler assembles these processes into a *work group* by creating an internal communication group within MPI. A request that is currently handled is called a *task*, and each work group is designated to compute one task. In order to manage this work group in a de-centralized way, the scheduler also creates a *task controller* instance in its own process that is part of the work group. While this task controller manages internal communication and state handling, the actual computation is done on the worker nodes.

Each worker node creates an instance of the same *command*, which in turn implements a parallel scheduling strategy, the actual visualization computation algorithm and a data transmission strategy. This command is executed in a separate thread, which enables the worker control flow to receive messages and to manage state handling. Each task is decomposed into a collection of subtasks that can be distributed among the available worker nodes. The typical sequence of operation is loading data, execution of a visualization algorithm and transmission of the result data to the ViSTA FlowLib client. Two data transmission strategies are typically used in Viracocha, direct transmission and the Master-Worker strategy [39]. The direct transmission strategy opens a TCP/IP network connection and transmits the result data directly to the requesting client. The Master-Worker strategy waits for the first worker to finish computation. This worker node then collects result data from all worker nodes that finish later and transmits this data using a single TCP/IP connection to the client.

Because Viracocha typically deals with large data, a data management layer was integrated [40]. This data management layer primarily caches previously loaded data and tries to prefetch future data requests. Several cache removal strategies and prefetching strategies are available. Prefetching is implemented in a separate data management thread, in order to overlap the loading operations with the algorithm execution in the command thread.

7.3. Improving Computation of Time-Varying Visualizations

Due to its flexible structure, various parallel algorithms can be implemented using Viracocha. In particular, multiple time-independent visualization algorithms have already been realized based on the basic Viracocha as described in Section 7.2. These time-independent problems are decomposed in a data parallel scheme where each time step is a single subtask. The applied scheduling strategy is a static decomposition of the set of all discrete time steps, which is either a decomposition into equally sized blocks or a Round-Robin scheme. For each assigned discrete time step, the command loads the necessary data, executes the visualization algorithm and uses a data transmission strategy to return the computed result to the ViSTA FlowLib client. Because the results for individual time steps can be computed independently, no interprocess-communication to compute the visualization is necessary.

Although data parallel computation of independent time steps is conceptually trivial, in practice a straightforward implementation as implemented in the basic version of Viracocha has multiple drawbacks, which impede software development and performance. We are going to detail these drawbacks in the following sections and introduce enhancements that we integrated into Viracocha to remedy these shortcomings for time-independent visualization tasks.

We separated the description of these improvements into performance-related improvements and flexibility (software construction)-related improvements. The former are beneficial for the visualization user—i.e., the simulation scientist who investigates data—, while the latter ease code development for the visualization tool developer.

7.3. IMPROVING COMPUTATION OF TIME-VARYING VISUALIZATIONS

7.3.1. Improving Performance

The major goal of using a parallel system is to improve performance [28]. In the context of this thesis, we measure performance by the time taken to compute a certain visualization request. In order to achieve high scalability, extra work due to the parallel system architecture needs to be reduced. This includes the extra effort to initialize the parallel system, to manage the processors, and to return results in a distributed system. We identified three major causes for reduced performance when computing time-independent visualizations using Viracocha: the overhead associated with the creation of a new task, the overhead due to returning result data in the client-server architecture, and the visualization algorithm itself. In this section, we describe only the modification to the existing worker process implementation that targets the first cause. Because the two latter problems are technical problems and not relevant for the further reading, they are addressed in Appendix B.2.

The major overhead for task creation and task modification is caused by the fact that Viracocha's commands are *stateless* [41]. This means Viracocha treats each request as an independent computation that is unrelated to any previous request. Each incoming request creates a new task and therefore new commands on each assigned worker. In addition, the full information to describe a task is transmitted every time (e.g., a complete data set description or a non-uniform sampling). If a request differs only in a minor parameter change to a previous request (e.g., changing the isovalue for a contour extraction command), this request causes unnecessary computational overhead to create the work group and instantiate the necessary objects. Moreover, possibly mandatory metadata like search structures have to be re-generated upon each request. This stateless execution of commands leads to additional overhead that decreases overall performance and in particular affects system responsiveness and request latency.

To remedy this shortcoming, we changed the underlying paradigm and transformed the stateless commands into *stateful* commands. That is, each command is in a defined state that determines the commands' behavior. Four possible states are assigned to a command: *init*, *processing*, *wait_for_update* and *finished*. A new command that is created starts in the *init* state. In this state, object construction and initialization that needs to be done only once is executed. When the initialization phase is completed, the command starts *processing* the task. It stays in state *processing* as long as uncomputed subtasks are available or the user explicitly stops the computation. Each worker processes its list of time steps asynchronously—that is, subtask processing is not synchronized among workers—, which increases performance. After all assigned time steps are computed, the command changes into the state *wait_for_update*. In this state, the command can either be *finished* or it receives a new request and returns to state *processing*. In state *finished*, the command is deleted and the work group disbanded. Thereafter, a subsequent request will again create a new work group and new commands.

107

CHAPTER 7. A PARALLEL SYSTEM FOR TIME-VARYING VISUALIZATIONS

This enhancement of a command by execution states enables a certain degree of persistence of a request. The loop introduced by the transition from *wait_for_update* back to *processing* enables the reuse of initialized objects and metadata. The benefit gained by stateful commands is based on the following assumption about user behavior: users more often adjust a small set of parameters than change to a totally different set of parameters or another visualization method. Several other visualization techniques are also based on this observation, for instance Differential Time-Histogram Tables [113].

7.3.2. Improving Flexibility

For the integration of new time-independent visualization algorithms or the modification of existing commands, we identified the existing *command* as a major flaw. The combination of scheduling, visualization algorithm and data transmission into a single command leads to code duplication. The same scheduling algorithm (e.g., Round-Robin distribution) or transmission protocol (e.g., MasterWorker strategy) is implemented in multiple commands, which only differ in the utilized visualization algorithm. Additionally, in order to change the scheduling algorithm or transmission protocol, a new command with an identical visualization algorithm has to be created. This approach leads to unnecessary programming effort and error-prone software maintenance.

To increase flexibility and enable code reuse, we separated the existing command into exchangeable scheduling, visualization algorithm and data transmission modules (see Figure 7.2). For the extracted scheduling module we chose a *strategy design pattern* [38] to implement different instances—that is, different scheduling strategies—of this module. A scheduling strategy communicates with the visualization algorithm using a task queue that contains information about the discrete time steps that have to be computed. The new scheduling component's responsibility is to fill this task queue according to the implemented scheduling behavior and the task description. In Section 7.4 we are going to describe multiple scheduling strategies. Here, we directly exploit the restriction that only time-independent visualization algorithm are considered. The visualization algorithm is executed using the first element (i.e., the first time step) in the task queue as input data, which is removed from the queue after computation. The execution is repeated until the task queue is empty.

In order to realize the extracted data transmission module we chose not to use the same *strategy design pattern* [38], but to decompose data transmission into smaller components. The reason is that we identified several code fragments to occur in multiple transmission modules, for instance merging and gathering of data or addition of metadata. To this end, we model the new data transmission strategy by a DataLaViSTA pipeline [8]. DataLaViSTA is a pipes-and-filters architecture that processes data in a packet-based way in order to transform or aggregate this data. The basic

7.3. IMPROVING COMPUTATION OF TIME-VARYING VISUALIZATIONS

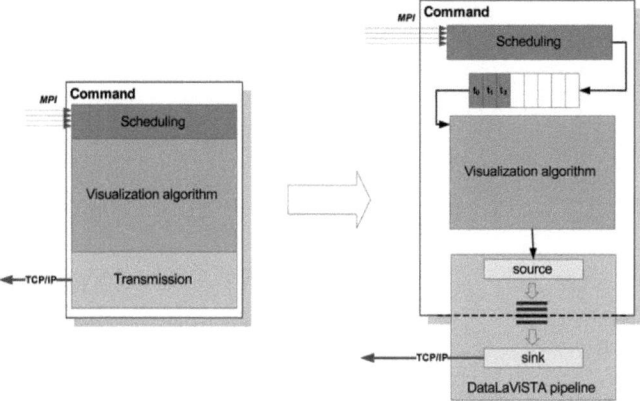

Figure 7.2.: Changed software structure of the Viracocha command: the scheduling, visualization algorithm, and data transmission code fragments that were united in a command (left) have been extracted into own modules (right). A task queue is employed for communication between scheduling and visualization algorithm. The DataLaViSTA pipes-and-filters architecture is employed to define transmission strategies. An arbitrary data flow between the source component (light yellow) and the queue (blue) can be defined. All data in the queue is transmitted by the sink component to the client.

idea of using this architecture to define the data transmission strategy is to replace the strategy by a modifiable pipeline description. This pipeline consists of reusable data transformation filters (e.g., stamp data packets) and data aggregation filters (e.g., merge data packets). Data is transported encapsulated in packets from a data producing source component to a data consuming sink component, with arbitrary filters in-between. The advantage of this procedure is that frequently occuring steps in the data transmission module are isolated in filters and can be used in nearly arbitrary combination with other filters.

Figure 7.2 shows the new data transmission structure. The only pre-defined parts of this pipeline are the data source (which is the interface to the visualization algorithm) and a queue that finally collects all data packets that need to be sent to the client (after their processing by the pipeline). Inbetween those two elements an arbitrary data flow can be defined. The transmission itself is done by a data consuming sink, which actively sends results to the client when result data is available in the queue. The function of the data queue and in particular the data sink is going to be detailed in Appendix B.2. An example to gather data in a single worker node using reusable filters is depicted in Figure 7.3.

This separation of scheduling, visualization algorithm, and data transmission enables a flexible combination of all three components. It eases the integration of new visualization algorithms into Viracocha, as the visualization developer does not have to deal with communication issues

109

CHAPTER 7. A PARALLEL SYSTEM FOR TIME-VARYING VISUALIZATIONS

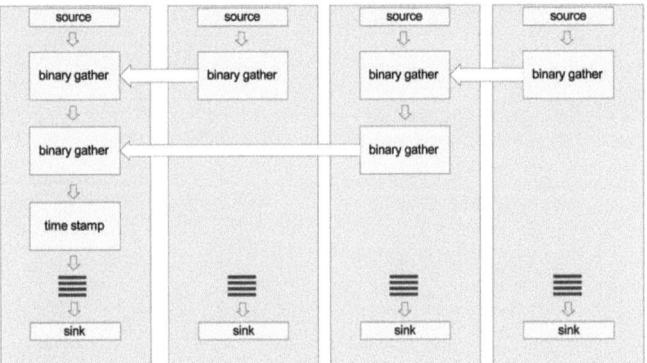

Figure 7.3.: Example of a possible transmission strategy built from existing filters: *binary gather* filters are arranged to gather data in a tree-wise fashion. All collected data is modified in a *time stamp* filter, before it is passed on to the data queue. All other worker nodes do not pass any data to their queue, because it is priorly re-routed by the *binary gather* filters.

(i.e., task scheduling and data transmission). In the same manner, a system developer can add new scheduling algorithms and transmission protocols without modifying existing visualization algorithms.

7.4. Scheduling Strategies

The assignment of subtasks to processes is a fundamental part in the parallelization of a computational problem. The primary performance goals of this assignment are to reduce interprocess communication, to balance the workload and to reduce the managing overhead for the assignment itself [28]. In the following text, we are going to use the terms assignment and scheduling interchangeably.

For data parallel computation of independent time steps interprocess communication between worker nodes is negligible. Therefore we focus on load balancing and overhead characteristics of scheduling strategies only. Two basic categories of scheduling techniques are distinguished: *static* and *dynamic* scheduling strategies. Static scheduling strategies do not incur much managing overhead during runtime because their assignment is predetermined. Dynamic scheduling adapts the task assignment at runtime and is therefore able to react to unexpected load imbalance. This dynamic behavior comes with the cost of higher managing overhead, as additional computation and communication is required to flexibly assign tasks.

For certain tasks, static strategies generate a sufficiently good load balancing, but in general

7.4. SCHEDULING STRATEGIES

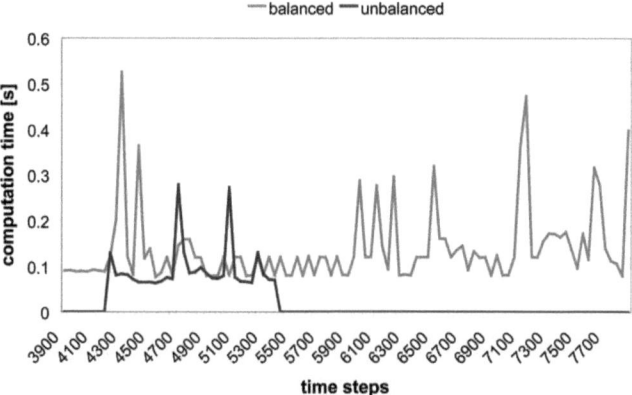

Figure 7.4.: Computation time for a contour visualization using the nasal airflow data set, shown for each 20th time step. Two different requests are shown, a *balanced* and an *unbalanced* request. Both requests differ in a single parameter, which describes the iso-value for which a contour geometry is computed. The balanced task contains an iso-value that is contained in all time steps and requires similar work on each discrete time step—only single peaks in the distribution point to small imbalances. The unbalanced task contains an iso-value that is only contained in a fraction of the time-varying data set. In the latter case, no computation is necessary for a large amount of time steps, which can lead to a significant load imbalance.

they do not [28]. Because arbitrary visualization algorithms on arbitrary simulation data can be executed using Viracocha, the work distribution in general often is too unpredictable. Figure 7.4 shows an example of the load distribution among discrete time steps for two different parameters of the same visualization technique. This example illustrates that the amount of work generated by a request may significantly vary even for small parameter changes.

In order to influence the computational order of subtasks when using a dynamic scheduling, we utilize a non-preemptive priority scheme. The scheduling algorithm assigns a priority rank to each subtask, and subtasks are arranged in order of their priority. However, unlike in many operating systems, incoming subtasks with higher priority do not interrupt running lower priority computations (non-preemptive). In the following, we are going to denote the rank of a subtask by the ranking function R (or prioritization function). Subtasks with a low rank R are assigned before subtasks with a high rank. Changing the computational order of subtasks is in certain cases useful to improve performance (see Section 7.4.1). In addition, because computed results are directly displayed to the user in an interactive animation, by changing the order of subtasks we can support the user's current analysis goal (see Section 7.4.2). Based on the changes in the software structure described in Section 7.3, the described scheduling strategies can be used in combination with arbitrary time-independent visualization algorithms.

CHAPTER 7. A PARALLEL SYSTEM FOR TIME-VARYING VISUALIZATIONS

7.4.1. Performance-Centered Scheduling

The primary goal of common scheduling strategies is to improve parallel performance, in particular to reduce the overall computation time. The static scheduling assumes an already load-balanced task distribution and avoids generating overhead, while dynamic strategies try to improve performance by an improved load balancing that is adapted during runtime. The static scheduling already available in Viracocha distributes equally sized chunks to each worker node. That is, for n time steps and p processors, each worker node is assigned a consecutive chunk of $\left\lfloor \frac{n}{p} \right\rfloor$ time steps. The remainder is distributed among the first processes. In addition to this existing static strategy, we integrated several dynamic strategies into Viracocha, which are described in the following text.

Multiple strategies to implement a dynamic scheduling strategy are possible. Because a dedicated task controller already manages a work group, we decided to utilize dynamic scheduling strategies managed by a centralized unit [78]. Such a centralized unit that coordinates workers has the disadvantage that every process accesses the same task queue, which potentially causes worker nodes to contend for new subtasks. The alternative are distributed queues—i.e., each worker has a task queue and "steals" subtasks from other workers to balance the computation. Though, a distributed coordination complicates prioritization strategies such as we are going to introduce in the next section.

That is, our dynamic scheduling strategies operate in the following way: each worker node that has currently no time steps to compute informs the central task controller. The task controller assigns the requesting worker a list—called *chunk* [28]—of m time steps to compute. After these m subtasks have been computed, the worker asks the task controller for a new chunk of subtasks to compute. We call such a strategy a *dynamic(m)*-strategy. The choice of m is a trade-off between subtask granularity and generated overhead. For instance, the *dynamic(1)*-strategy allows the most fine-grained assignment of subtasks, but generates substantial overhead because communication between worker and task controller is necessary for each subtask.

An approach to adapt the chunk size m during scheduling was proposed by Polychronopoulos and Kuck [78]. As part of their guided self-scheduling strategy, they proposed to decrease the amount of work that is assigned to workers continuously. That is, while at the beginning larger chunks are distributed to the worker nodes, the last subtasks are assigned in small chunks to achieve a better trade-off between overhead and subtask granularity. The chunk size m is determined in each assignment step i by the following operation. Let $X_1 = n$, where n is the number of time steps that make-up the task, and p the number of worker processes. Then $m_i = \left\lceil \frac{X_i}{p} \right\rceil$. After each step i, the number of remaining tasks X_{i+1} in the next step is decreased by the amount of assigned tasks m_i: $X_{i+1} = X_i - m_i$. In the following, this strategy is denoted by *dynamic(g)*,

7.4. SCHEDULING STRATEGIES

where g means guided scheduling.

For computation tasks that involve intensive file I/O, dynamic scheduling exhibits another disadvantage. The Viracocha system's data management caches once used data in order to avoid recurring file I/O. Because Viracocha supports distributed memory systems, the data management stores cached data locally at each process. By dynamically assigning time steps to worker nodes, it is likely that in subsequent tasks the same time step is assigned to different worker nodes, thereby negating the benefits of the cache. Therefore, we propose to modify the *dynamic(g)*-scheduling strategy such that it respects the cache's content.

This is done by ranking each subtask according to the content of the distributed caches. More specifically, when a new list of m subtasks has to be assigned to a worker node, not the first m subtasks in the task queue are assigned, but a set of m subtasks with the lowest rank values R. We assume that the task queue contains k subtasks $d_{i_0}, \ldots, d_{i_{k-1}}$. Then, the cache-aware ranking function R for worker w is given by

$$R(w, d_{i_j}) = \begin{cases} j & \text{if requesting worker } w \text{ has } d_{i_j} \text{ in its cache,} \\ k & \text{if } d_{i_j} \text{ is not cached at any worker,} \\ k+1 & \text{if another worker } v \neq w \text{ has } d_{i_j} \text{ in its cache.} \end{cases}$$

The information of the workers' cache content is provided by the data management system. Using this prioritization, first subtasks that require already cached data are assigned to the requesting worker, and these subtasks remain in their original order in the task queue. Thereafter, subtasks that require new data, which is not cached at any other worker node, are chosen. Finally, subtasks that involve data already loaded by other workers are assigned. This adapted strategy is denoted by *dynamic (g,c)*, where c means cache-prioritization.

An alternative of *dynamic (g,c)* is to prohibit the last case, that is a worker cannot "steal" subtasks that require already loaded data from other worker nodes. While this increases the processing time of such a subtask—because the scheduling will always wait for a specific worker to be finished—it is beneficial if memory is limited or the data specified by the subtasks is very I/O-expensive.

These variants of dynamic scheduling target reduction of the overall computation time. While parallel computation time influences the user's waiting time significantly, the order in which subtasks are computed also affects perceived waiting times. In the next section, we are going to introduce scheduling strategies that in particular target reduction of the user's waiting time.

CHAPTER 7. A PARALLEL SYSTEM FOR TIME-VARYING VISUALIZATIONS

7.4.2. User-Centered Scheduling

High overall performance is desirable because it decreases the user's waiting time between sending the request and receiving the entire result data. But, in this section we are going to show that the user's waiting time to answer an analysis question is not equivalent to the time span required to compute the time-varying visualization.

For the computation of time-varying visualization data, the result data comprises a set of discrete visualizations, each of which is valid for a single time step. When using the direct transmission strategy, the resulting visualization for each discrete time step is immediately sent to the client, that is partial results are already displayed to the user. The ViSTA FlowLib client utilizes an *interactive animation* display representation of the time-varying visualization (cp. Section 4.3.1). That is, at each point in time the user sees the visualization of a single time step only. This implies that the waiting time of the user depends on the order in which subtasks are computed. For example, if the user had stopped the animation and the currently visible time step would be the last one that is computed, the waiting time equals the overall computation time. If this time step were computed first, waiting time would obviously be shorter independent of the overall waiting time—of course, only if more than one time step is requested.

In general, in order to answer a specific analysis question, the user requires a set of discrete visualization data that sufficiently describes the desired part of the simulation data w.r.t. the analysis goal. Besides overall response time, we define a more abstract type of waiting time: the user's perceived waiting time. The *perceived waiting time* is the time span between the time instant the user issues a visualization request and the point in time the computed (potentially only partial) result is sufficient to decide if the generated visualization answers the user's problem. As an example, we describe the following scenario:

> An engineer searches for vortex structures in a time-varying simulation of the flow around an aircraft. He adapts a single parameter λ_2 to visualize vortex structures and first tries to find a suitable λ_2 value. Until such a value is found, the engineer repeatedly requests visualizations for different λ_2 values and each time investigates the time-varying visualization if the chosen parameter clearly defines the vortex structures. Once such a value is found, the engineer repeatedly observes the time-varying vortex structures to identify regions of interest, while he will fine-tune the chosen parameter. Eventually, he finds a vortex shedding, stops the animation, and analyzes this phenomena with other visualization techniques in combination with maneuver movements.

In this scenario, the user has three goals in a sequence: find a good λ_2 value, find interesting

7.4. SCHEDULING STRATEGIES

regions by fine-tuning this value, and a detailed analysis of a single vortex. This scenario matches the task analysis described in Section 4.2. The user's perceived waiting time depends on the current analysis goal, which may change during the analysis process—as demonstrated in the example. Under these assumptions, a scheduling that reduces the time until a user can achieve his current goal is obviously superior to other computation schedules. However, a computer cannot directly identify the user's current goal (sometimes, even users are unable to identify their goal) and it cannot decide if a visualization is significant to answer a question. We therefore rely on an explicit statement by the user about the current analysis goal. We introduce the term *user-centered scheduling* for all scheduling strategies that incorporate the user's analysis goals w.r.t. temporal navigation.

Based on the task analysis elaborated in Section 4.2, in this section we propose three scheduling strategies: *overview*, *continuous visualization* and *local investigation*. Each strategy tries to reduce the perceived waiting time for a particular analysis goal that is linked to some temporal interaction. These strategies are based on the *dynamic(1)* strategy in order have a fine-granular control of the computational order. This allows to adapt the strategies to changing user behavior during computation. Another conceptual difference is, that these strategies do not rank time steps directly, but the corresponding time indices. This is because the interactive animation displays time steps in the order of their indices. A time step is assigned the lowest rank from all time indices that point to this time step.

7.4.2.1. Overview Strategy

During the exploration phase (see Section 4.2), the goal of the investigating user is to get an overview of the visualized simulation. One common behavior is to vary visualization parameters and to observe the overall effect on the animated time-varying visualization. That is, for each parameter change the user would like to quickly judge if the change has a desired effect on the entire time-varying visualization.

We assume that the temporal sampling that describes the time-varying data already resolves important regions sufficiently high, and unimportant regions are resolved only coarsely. Hence, available importance definitions are not used to determine the computational order. Rather we try to produce a fast overview of the given (possibly non-uniform) sampling.

In order to support this user task, we subsample the shown time-varying visualization using a decreasing sample rate. But, instead of subsampling the available discrete sampling as done in Chapter 6, we sample the visible simulation time range. This results in an equally distributed sampling along the visualized phenomenon instead of an equally distributed sampling along the available time steps. In particular for a non-uniform sampled temporal resolution this distinction makes a major difference.

Let p be the number of available worker nodes. For a simulation interval of size Δs, we start with a sample rate $s_0 = \frac{\Delta s}{p}$ and sample continuously along the visible simulation time interval. We chose a sample rate that is a multiple of the available number of workers to obtain a good load balancing during the first steps. Now, in each step k, this rate is decreased by $s_{k+1} = \frac{s_k}{2}$. We proceed using this algorithm until all time steps are covered. The time steps corresponding to a sample position obtained by s_k are collected in the set S_k. This algorithm is summarized in Algorithm 3.

Algorithm 3 Overview Ranking

Require: size of simulation time interval $s_{end} - s_{start} = \Delta s$
Require: number of available worker nodes p
1: init sampling rate $s_0 = \frac{\Delta s}{p}$
2: init $k = 0$
3: **while** not all time steps covered **do**
4:    init sample position $s = s_{start} + \frac{s_k}{2}$
5:    **while** $s < s_{end}$ **do**
6:       add time step $d = \hat{i} \circ \hat{s}(s)$ to list S_k
7:    **end while**
8:    $s_{k+1} = \frac{s_k}{2}$
9:    $k = k + 1$
10: **end while**
11: return $S_0, \ldots, S_{k-1}$

Now, we apply a ranking function that evaluates the first sample rate at which a time step d_j was touched:

$$R(d_j) = \operatorname{argmin}_i (d_j \in S_i).$$

This consecutive sampling forms an order on all discrete time steps of the requested temporal sampling. The idea is, that the sampling is subsequently refined until the whole sampling is shown. Figure 7.5 illustrates the desired computing order. At any point in time, the user can abort the computation and modify his request.

7.4.2.2. Continuous Visualization Strategy

During the search phase (see Section 4.2), a common goal is to analyze the dynamic characteristics of a phenomenon that is possibly of interest. To investigate the time-varying properties of the phenomenon, the user is interested in a continuous animation of the time-varying visualization.

7.4. SCHEDULING STRATEGIES

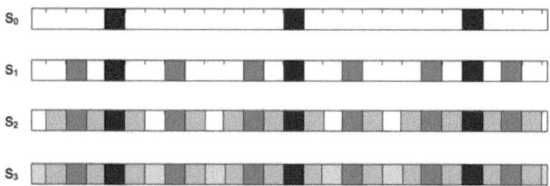

Figure 7.5.: Exemplary sequence of the overview scheduling. Colored boxes represent ranked time steps. The time interval is sampled using a decreasing sample rate, and time steps are ranked according to the highest sample rate that touched them. The result is an ordering that first coarsely samples the data (S_0), and then successively refines the shown resolution ($S_1 - S_2$), until all time steps are computed (S_3).

During the animation, he will fine-tune or modify the visualization's parameter. Visible gaps in this animation—that is, time steps for which data has yet to be computed while the animation passes the corresponding time interval—are undesirable to convey the dynamic qualities of the time-varying visualization.

In order to achieve this goal, two problems need to be solved:

1. How fast can the animation be displayed while continuously computing visualization data, limited by the available parallel resources?

2. Which subtasks should be requested when?

Concerning the first question, we are going to examine the request and compute processes using a simplified statistical model. To this end, we model the Viracocha system as a queuing system with a single queue [26]. Queuing systems are characterized by an arrival process, a service time distribution, the number of servers and the buffer size to store requests. The arrival process describes how the interarrival times between two subsequent requests are distributed; the service time distribution describes the distribution of service times, analogously.

To model the arrival process, we describe the following process for this usage scenario: the animation is running, we assume a uniformally distributed subsampling, and each discrete time step is shown in the animation for t_{frame} seconds. This value t_{frame} is not to be mistaken with the rendering time for a single image. During a display time t_{frame}, this time step's visualization is typically rendered multiple times. Whenever a new time step is shown, a new time step is requested from the server. That is, the interarrival rate of requests is deterministic and is given by $\lambda = \frac{1}{t_{frame}}$. Requests comprise a single time step only. The server needs in average $\bar{t}_{comp}$ to manage and compute each time step; the service rate is given by $\mu = \frac{1}{\bar{t}_{comp}}$. The service times t_{comp} for each individual time step are typically not deterministic but are influenced by task imbalance and system load. However, here we assume deterministic service times—that is, each time step requires $\bar{t}_{comp}$ to be computed—for the sake of simplicity. Deterministic service times can be safely assumed if all time steps require the same amount of time to compute (i.e., the subtasks are balanced or each subtask is computed with a predefined time budget) and random system effects do not influence computation time significantly. We are going to discuss the non-deterministic cases at the end of this section. The buffer size to store requests is infinite, because the task queue's size is not restricted.

Such a serial system can be described using Kendall's notation [26] by a $D/D/1$ queue, that is deterministic arrival, deterministic service, and a single service process. The task queue's content of a $D/D/1$ system constantly grows if $\lambda > \mu$ [118]. This is intuitive, as requests arrive quicker than they are computed. In the case $\lambda < \mu$, the system is stable, as either currently a task is computed or the system is idle. This is equal to $t_{frame} > \bar{t}_{comp}$, that is the animation shows visualizations slower than the time required to compute them.

The parallel Viracocha system can now be characterized using Kendall's notation by a $D/D/p$ queue, that is deterministic arrival, deterministic service, and p worker nodes. This queue is stable if $\lambda < p\mu$ (this also holds for $\lambda = p\mu$ in a special case that is not discussed here) [118].

This model shows, that for a number of processors p and a computation rate of $\mu = \frac{1}{\bar{t}_{comp}}$ time steps per second, the animation rate $\lambda = \frac{1}{t_{frame}}$ time steps per seconds should be chosen such that

$$\frac{\lambda}{\mu} < p \iff \frac{\bar{t}_{comp}}{t_{frame}} < p.$$

When a user requests a visualization using the continuous visualization strategy, the animation rate is adapted by the system to match this requirement (automatic speed selection, see Section 4.2). Of course, if the current animation speed is sufficient to provide a continuous visualization given the available resources, no adaption is necessary. On the other hand, a too long animation time t_{frame} is unacceptable, because the resulting animation is no longer perceived as a continuous process. According to Bryson [16], data should change at least every $\frac{1}{3}$ seconds. A low number of available processors p and a long average computation time $\bar{t}_{comp}$ possibly result in a necessary animation time t_{frame} that exceeds this threshold. In Wolter et. al. [108], we have proposed to introduce an additional buffer time—a technique similar to buffering in video streaming. By increasing the waiting time to the first visible result, the difference between animation and computation time can be reduced to a certain degree. However, for a computation time of a minute or more, the sufficient amount of parallel resources is typically not available and the necessary buffer is too long for interactive usage. In this case, a meaningful continuous vsiualization cannot be provided. The only solution to this problem is to reduce the computation time for each single subtask, for instance, by hybrid parallelization [110].

7.4. SCHEDULING STRATEGIES

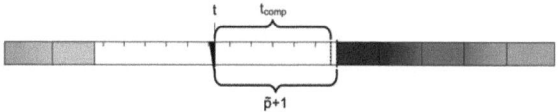

Figure 7.6.: Sketch of the continuous visualization strategy. The time step that becomes visible first, after the estimated computation time, is computed first. Subsequent time steps are computed by and by.

The second question concerns the subtasks that should be requested at a specific point in time during the animation. Beforehand, we introduce the function $\hat{u}^* : U \to P$ that is defined by the concatenation of all mappings from user time to time steps: $\hat{u}^*(t) = \hat{i} \circ \hat{s} \circ \hat{v} \circ \hat{u}(t)$ (see Section 3.3). This function $\hat{u}^*$ maps each specific user time to the corresponding discrete time step.

Because in general $t_{frame} < \bar{t}_{comp}$ holds, a request issued at user time t should not contain the time step $p = \hat{u}^*(t)$. This is because the computation is finished at $t + \bar{t}_{comp}$, but the time step is shown in the animation just until $t + t_{frame} < t + \bar{t}_{comp}$. The produced data only becomes visible to the user in the next animation loop, which results in an increased waiting time for this time step.

Therefore, the requested data at user time t should be chosen such that it becomes immediately visible after $t + \bar{t}_{comp}$. For a request issued at t, the time step that is shown at the arrival time of this request's result is $\tilde{p} = \hat{u}^*(t + \bar{t}_{comp})$. At the point in time at which the result data is available, the animation has possibly shown a part of the simulation time interval associated with $\tilde{p}$, therefore $\tilde{p}$ is possibly visible shorter than t_{frame}. In order to present the result time for the entire available animation time t_{frame}, the next time step $\tilde{p} + 1$ is requested instead of only $\tilde{p}$. This strategy is depicted in Figure 7.6.

It should be noted that while this strategy results in a continuous animation, it does not enable interactive parameter changes. A parameter change has consequences in the animation after $\bar{t}_{comp}$ at the earliest. To enable interactive parameter changes in time-varying data, we proposed dynamic region-of-interests (DROI) [106], which are based on this continuous visualization scheduling strategy. Instead of computing the visualization, the worker nodes compute a simplified region-of-interest that surrounds the user's input device and which position is predicted $\bar{t}_{comp}$ into the future. The data for each time step arrives before the animation shows this time step, and a visualization based on the user's input device (e.g., a cutplane) is computed interactively within the resampled region. However, this technique is not analyzed in the context of this thesis.

The applied queuing model uses multiple simplifications. A deterministic arrival time distribution is only a valid assumption for discrete time steps that possess uniform simulation time values. While this assumption is often correct, the service time distribution is typically not deterministic. However, using the worst occuring computation time for $\bar{t}_{comp}$ results in a pessimistic, but deterministic value. Another solution is to use time-critical computation to keep the computation time on different time steps constant. Non-deterministic effects from system randomness cannot be eliminated entirely, but using an idle system reduces random side-effects from other jobs. In addition to a deterministic computation time, the queuing model assumes that scheduling and parallelizing costs no time, which does not hold in practice. Service time depends on the number of workers, which should be incorporated by using the measured speed-up as k, and not the number of available processors. And last, queuing theory describes the average system state or the system's state in equilibrium with $t \to \infty$. In the Viracocha system, the number of received requests is finite. However, for a large number of discrete time steps we assume that these statements still hold.

In summary, the continuous visualization strategy tries to minimize the additional waiting time between reception and display of a visualization. By automatic adaption of animation speed based on the available number of worker nodes and prediction of future result arrival times, this strategy enables a continuous animation of time-varying visualizations. Queuing theory gives us a tool to determine the maximum animation rate at which a given number of processors can continuously compute visualizations. Visible gaps in the animation are avoided if the computation time estimations are correct. An additional benefit of this scheduling technique is, that it does not depend on the number of discrete time steps. It correlates computation and animation speed and is therefore usable with an arbitrary number of time steps.

7.4.2.3. Local Investigation Strategy

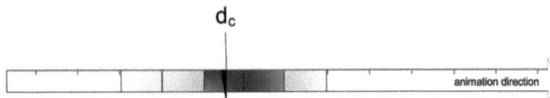

Figure 7.7.: Priority of time steps when a user pauses the animation to investigate a time step and its local neighborhood. The focussed time step obtains highest priority, neighboring time steps are assigned lower priorities. Time steps in line with the animation direction receive higher priorities.

Once the domain scientist has found a phenomenon of interest, this temporally local part of the data is analyzed in the focus phase (see Section 4.2). Maneuvering travel interaction is generally applied to investigate a point in time or a short sequence in more detail. That is, the user has stopped the animation to analyze the properties of each single time step. If the user is also interested in the dynamics of that phenomenon, he will examine the temporal environment around this time step by slow travel actions to close targets (e.g., stepping forward or backward in time).

In order to support this focused investigation on the time step d_c, we utilize the following ranking function R:

$$R(d_{i_j}) = \begin{cases} |d_{i_j} - d_c| & \text{if } d_{i_j} \text{ is in the direction of animation,} \\ |d_{i_j} - d_c| + k_{dir} & \text{else.} \end{cases}$$

with $0 < k_{dir} < 1$ to penalize time steps before the current time step d_c in the animation. Whenever the animation is stopped, the current time step is assigned the highest priority (i.e., lowest R). All other time steps are marked with a priority according to their distance to d_c (see Figure 7.7). Time step neighbours in the same direction as the animation get a higher priority than neighbors in the opposite direction. This ensures that more time steps are available in the direction of the animation when the animation is resumed.

Two types of updates are relevant for this strategy: visualization parameter updates and maneuver movements. When the user changes a visualization parameter that requires a recomputation of the visualization, only the focussed time step and its neighborhood are recomputed. The size of this neighborhood m is typically user-determined and depends on the temporal extent of the phenomenon under investigation. As a default value we propose to use a multiple of the number of available worker nodes, because this ensures a good load balancing of the resulting request and exploits the available resources. When the user executes a maneuver movement—that is, he steps single time steps forward or backward in time—the currently visible time step is chosen as the focussed one. This results in a computation of the current visualization for the time steps that are now within the neighborhood radius m.

In summary, the time a user takes to examine a certain time step is used to compute the temporal environment around that time step. The (scheduled) computational order depends on the distance to the current focus time instant. When the user decides to maneuver forwards or backwards in time, the appropriate data is likely available depending on the time he spent analyzing the focused time step.

7.5. Results

The main goal of this chapter is to exploit the computational power provided by parallel computing as an effective countermeasure against the increasing temporal resolution of simulation data (see Section 7.1). Though, the achievable specific scalability significantly depends on the used visualization algorithm, the analyzed data set, and the utilized parallel machine, which cannot be evaluated extensively in the context of this thesis. Therefore, we follow a two-step approach: first, we present previous results that have been achieved using the improved Viracocha system in

CHAPTER 7. A PARALLEL SYSTEM FOR TIME-VARYING VISUALIZATIONS

Section 7.5.1. Second, in Sections 7.5.2 to 7.5.5 we use a single data set and the same visualization technique in order to compare the characteristics of different approaches we have described.

The used data set is the nasal airflow simulation (see Section C.1). To obtain comparable results, we apply the same visualization technique on this data set: a contour over a certain iso-value c was computed using VTK's contour filter [89]; point normals on the resulting geometry were determined using the *vtkPolyDataNormals* filter. In this evaluation, two parameters of this visualization were varied: the requested iso-value c and the size k of the temporal sampling. Concerning the former parameter, two distinct iso-values to generate different computational tasks were used. A density contour of the value $c = 0.92$ generated a *balanced* computational load among all time steps, because this value is contained in all time steps. That is, every time step required a comparable amount of work with single exceptions only (see Figure 7.4). A pressure contour of value $c = 0.632$ produced a highly *unbalanced* load distribution. This value was only contained in about a third of the time span, which resulted in a reduced amount of work for two thirds of the data (see Figure 7.4). While c can be used to vary the subtask balance, the sampling size k was used to vary the overall computational load.

The results presented in Sections 7.5.2 to 7.5.5 were measured on the same hardware system. Both the Viracocha application and the ViSTA FlowLib client were executed on a cluster of twelve Sun Ultra 40 M2 machines, each of which possesses two Dual Core Opteron 2.6 GHz processors, 8 GB main memory, and an NVIDIA Quadro FX 5600 graphics card. All machines were connected using a dedicated 1 GBit Ethernet. Data sets were stored on a file server equipped with a RAID-5 storage shared by all machines. Twelve machines were available; one node is required for the client, one for the scheduler process. Therefore, scalability measurements could be carried out with up to ten worker nodes. We used one, two, four and eight processors for scalability measurements, because this corresponds to the commonly shown double increase in resources.

We are going to use the following numbers to evaluate different aspects of the described techniques. The overall runtime r_{all} is the time measured on the client system between the issueing of the request and the reception of the last result that corresponds to this request. The time until the first result arrives r_{first} is the time measured on the client system between issuing the request and receiving the first result associated to this request. This number gives an impression of the system's update latency. The speedup S for n worker nodes is the ratio of the running time on a single processor $T(1)$ to the running time $T(n)$ on the parallel configuration. That is $S(n) = \frac{T(1)}{T(n)}$ [32]. Similar, parallel efficiency defined by $E(n) = \frac{S(n)}{n}$ is a measure for the exploitation of the used parallel processors.

7.5.1. Previous Results

The improved parallel system as described in this thesis has been successfully applied in a number of scientific visualization studies, whose results are reported here briefly. In Hentschel et al. [53, 54], we used Viracocha for brushing of time-varying data. We measured the overall computation time as well as the computation time until the first result arrived. *Static* scheduling was used, as all data was loaded beforehand into the workers' cache. A measurement on 48 time steps of an unstructured data set, which consumes approximatedly 26 GB disk space, achieved parallel efficiencies of around 80%. To further improve runtime as well as to reduce the waiting time until the first result appears, we parallelized the selection algorithm using OpenMP (see Section B.2). Using hybrid parallelization, the overall runtime r_{all} was reduced for this time-independent visualization from 24 s using a single processor to 2.7 s using eight processors and three threads. In another previous work, we have shown a similar parallel efficiency of 73-81% with up to 64 worker nodes on an SMP machine with 72 processors with a data set comprising 128 time steps (consuming 4 GB disk space) [108]. Here, overall runtime of a contour visualization has been reduced from 1044 s (17 minutes 24 seconds) using a single processor to 21 s using 64 processors. These results exemplarily show that parallel computation is an effective means to reduce overall runtimes for time-independent visualizations. In particular, overall runtimes can be reduced in a way that they belong to a different class of tolerable waiting times as defined by Miller [76]. For instance, waiting for 17 minutes inside a virtual environment is totally unacceptable, while 21 seconds is acceptable if the user can turn to other activities in the meantime. The same holds for a waiting time of 24 seconds, whereas 2.7 seconds is close to the amount of time users wait for routine requests [76].

7.5.2. Performance-Decreasing Effects

Despite the straightforward parallelization for time-independent visualization techniques, the measured parallel efficiencies were not optimal. Experience has shown that for computation of time-independent visualizations, file I/O and result transmission to the client are the most common bottlenecks [53, 54, 108]. Figure 7.8 shows the effects of file I/O and result transmission for a specific visualization computation. Scalability was measured for the balanced request comprising $k = 250$ time steps of the nasal airflow data set using *static* scheduling. The figure shows that scalability is limited even with only eight worker nodes if the command comprises file I/O, computation, and result transmission. If we omit result transmission to the client (which is of course not possible in our interactive usage scenario), scalability for computation + file I/O increases. Finally, omitting file I/O (which is made possible by Viracocha's data management) gives a further increase of scalability. For this parallel computation without file I/O and data transmission, a nearly optimal speed-up was achieved.

CHAPTER 7. A PARALLEL SYSTEM FOR TIME-VARYING VISUALIZATIONS

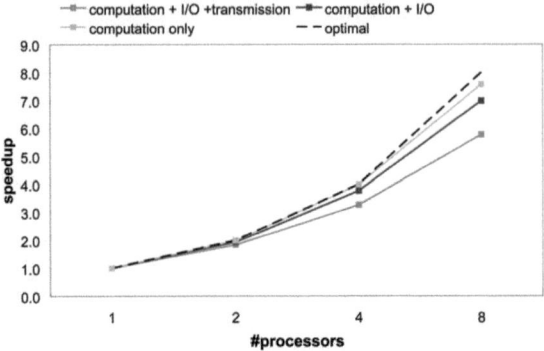

Figure 7.8.: The effect of file I/O and result transmission to the client on scalability. Speedup was measured with a balanced request comprising $k = 250$ time steps of the nasal airflow data set. Omitting both file I/O and result transmission significantly improves scalability, which identifies these two algorithm parts as bottlenecks.

Even though these results were obtained by an exemplary visualization computation, they correspond to measurements obtained by previous work. As a result, although decomposition of independent time steps is an embarrassingly parallel problem, file I/O from a shared file system and result transmission to a shared receiver can be identified as bottlenecks that decrease scalability.

7.5.3. Improving Performance

The performance gain by changing a stateless command into a stateful command depends on the initialization costs of the utilized command. In order to exemplarily show this effect for a specific command, we executed the balanced request with $k = 100$ using both a stateless and stateful command. Figure 7.9 compares the overall runtime r_{all} as well as the time until the first result is received by the client r_{first} for a parallel computation using eight worker nodes. Results show averaged values over ten identical requests. For the stateful command, the command was initialized before the measurement. Initialization of the used command comprised only the construction of the VTK pipeline, but no additional metadata. Data management was inactive, such that the presented runtimes do not include caching effects.

The results show that in this measurement, the stateful command is overall 1.2 s (from 4.9 s to 3.7 s, approx. 25%) faster than the stateless command, and the first result arrives 64 ms (from 300 ms to 236 ms, approx. 20%) earlier using the stateful command. Again, these specific numbers are obtained by an exemplary visualization request. The general performance gain significantly depends on the specific implementation of the used command. However, the results show exem-

7.5. RESULTS

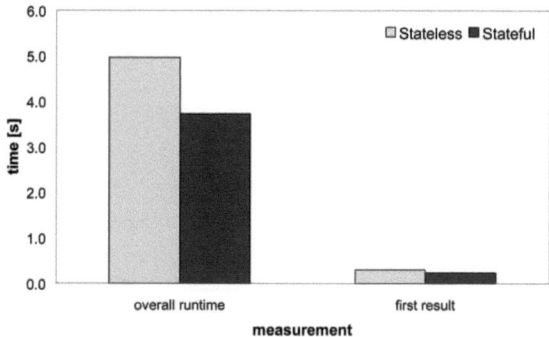

Figure 7.9.: Improvement of the Viracocha system by changing stateless commands into stateful commands measured by the overall runtime and the time until the first result is available.

plarily that by exploitation of similarity between subsequent requests, a considerable performance improvement can be achieved.

7.5.4. Performance-Centered Scheduling Strategies

To evaluate the newly integrated dynamic scheduling strategies, we utilize the described balanced and unbalanced requests using both $k = 100$ and $k = 250$ time steps. Eight worker nodes were employed to compute the requests. We measured the overall computation time until all results were received at the client. The shown values are averages from 20 measurements. In these measurements, the cache provided by Viracocha's data management was not utilized in order not to measure any caching effects. The results are shown in Figure 7.10.

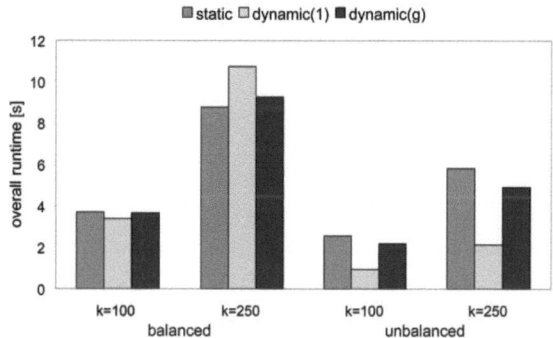

Figure 7.10.: Performance data for multiple scheduling strategies without Viracocha's data management.

125

CHAPTER 7. A PARALLEL SYSTEM FOR TIME-VARYING VISUALIZATIONS

For balanced requests, the *static* scheduling achieves good results. For small requests (i.e., $k = 100$), *dynamic (1)*-scheduling beats *static* scheduling for the balanced request. This is because even the balanced request is not fully balanced (see Figure 7.4), which is exploited by the *dynamic (1)*-scheduling. However, for the larger request (i.e., $k = 250$), the overhead produced by the fine-granular *dynamic (1)*-strategy leads to inferior runtimes. For unbalanced requests, the *dynamic(1)*-strategy clearly dominates all other strategies, because the additional overhead is compensated by the improved load balance. In both types of requests, the *guided*-scheduling provides similar results as the *static* scheduling, with slightly better performance in the unbalanced case.

In the previous measurement, we disabled Viracocha's data management to exclude caching effects and thereby to maintain comparability. However, the data management's cache can significantly influence computation time and is commonly used in realistic usage scenarios. Hence, we analyzed the cache's efficiency with respect to the used scheduling strategy and compared overall performance with cached data. To obtain comparable results, we assumed sufficient memory to keep the whole request data in the workers' caches. We computed the request once without measuring in order to fill the caches and then repeated the same request 20 times. Figure 7.11 shows the averaged overall runtime with activated cache and the average cache hits as percentage of the number of total requested time steps.

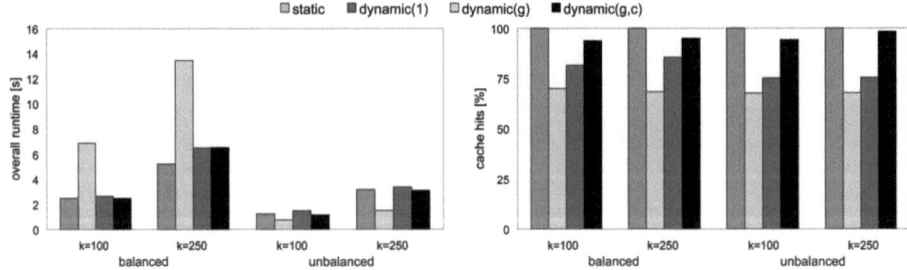

Figure 7.11.: Performance data for multiple scheduling strategies with activated caching. Left: Overall computation time for all time steps. Right: Cache hits in the Viracocha data management system for subsequent requests on the same data.

If all data fits into caches, the *static* scheduling that always assigns the same subtasks to the same workers achieves optimal cache efficiency (see Figure 7.11 right). In addition, this results in improved overall runtimes using *static* scheduling even for the unbalanced request, because the overall load is reduced. As expected, *dynamic(1)*-scheduling scores only a lower number of cache hits—approximately 70%—due to the dynamic assignment of subtasks to different worker nodes and therefore different cache contents. While still superior to other strategies for the unbalanced request, performance decreases significantly for the balanced request. Here, overall runtime with activated caching is even inferior compared to the overall runtime without caching. We explain

7.5. RESULTS

this effect by a reduced efficiency of harddisk and operating system caching, which could not be disabled in these measurements. We substantiate this presumption by an increased average file I/O time that was observed in the measurements with activated caching.

Dynamic (g)-scheduling assigns larger blocks of subtasks and therefore creates larger overlaps between subsequent requests, which increases the average cache hits to 75-80%. Nonetheless, the superior caching effects of the *static* scheduling result in slightly inferior overall performance for *dynamic (g)*-scheduling compared to *static* scheduling. By including the worker's cache into the ranking of subtasks using the *dynamic (g,c)*-strategy, the number of cache hits in subsequent requests can be increased to 95-98%. However, in the balanced request this does not have a significant effect, because the additional cache hits do not compensate the additional scheduling overhead. In the unbalanced request the benefit of dynamic assignment is higher, which in combination with a high number of cache hits reduces overall runtime below the time required using a *static* scheduling.

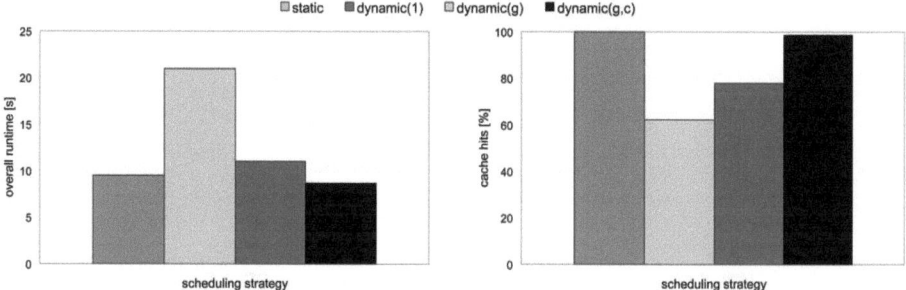

Figure 7.12.: Overall runtimes (left) and cache hits (right) for the blood pump data set.

In order to analyze the techniques with a different ratio between scheduling time and file I/O, Figure 7.12 shows the same measurement for a more I/O-intensive request. This request includes the same visualization technique, but computed with $k = 100$ time steps of the blood pump data set (see Section C.3). Caching was enabled for the measurements. These data set's time steps are five times larger on harddisk than the nasal airflow simulation's time steps, which results in longer file I/O times. Despite the different I/O load, results are similar to the nasal airflow use case.

7.5.5. User-Centered Scheduling Strategies

To evaluate the usefulness of the user-centered scheduling strategies, one needs to verify that these scheduling strategies decrease the user's perceived waiting time. But, to formulate a measurable

CHAPTER 7. A PARALLEL SYSTEM FOR TIME-VARYING VISUALIZATIONS

hypothesis, such an evaluation requires a user study with multiple domain-specific tasks in order to measure the achievement of defined analysis goals. Besides several domain scientists as subjects, several suitable simulation data sets are required to compare different analysis goals. Tasks have to be designed that do not significantly depend on knowledge disparities between subjects. Because the design and conduction of such a study would be extremely expensive, we decided to show only directly measureable data. While this gives a good indication of the usefulness of the proposed scheduling strategies, it does not fully replace the need of a comprehensive user study.

To depict the obtained computational order for each scheduling strategy, we plot the arrival time at the requesting client. More specifically, for each discrete time step the plot shows a vertical greyscale line whose color depicts the arrival time. Darker regions corresponds to an early arrival time, while brighter regions depict late arrival times. The resulting greyscale-charts show the entire arrival time distribution along the time step frame. Because the proposed user-centered strategies are based on the *dynamic (1)*-strategy, the same performance values as reported in the last section apply.

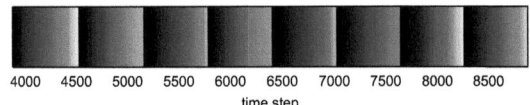

Figure 7.13.: Arrival distribution with *static* scheduling. Darker time steps arrive earlier than brighter ones.

Figure 7.13 shows the result arrival times for the *static* scheduling. From this greyscale-chart, the decomposition of the discrete time steps among the worker nodes is apparent. We utilized eight worker nodes, and each worker computes a contiguous set of time steps from left to right. It is apparent that the arrival distribution is solely determined by the applied computational strategy and does not take the user's analysis goal into consideration.

Overview Strategy

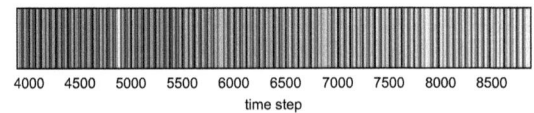

Figure 7.14.: Arrival distribution with *overview* scheduling. Darker time steps arrive earlier than brighter ones.

Figure 7.14 shows the result arrival times for an *overview* user-centered scheduling. Arrival times are distributed over the temporal domain. In particular, the first results that arrive (shown in black) are uniformly distributed among the simulation time frame. A slight brightness shift to the right is noticeable, that is later time steps tend to arrive later. This is explained by the growing size of the sets S_k with growing step number k. As soon as S_k is larger than the number of available worker nodes, a computation order within S_k is enforced. Because we sample from left to right, this order passes on to the computational order.

Continuous Visualization Strategy

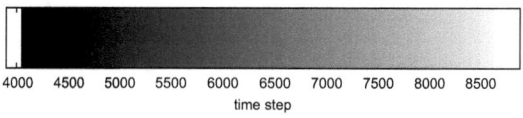

Figure 7.15.: Arrival distribution with *continuous* scheduling. Darker time steps arrive earlier than brighter ones.

Figure 7.15 shows the result arrival times for a *continuous* user-centered scheduling. Starting from the point in time the request started, the visualization is continuously built up from left to right. To evaluate this strategy, we define two additional visibility measures: waiting time to the first result and the number of visible gaps. The waiting time for the first visible result $\Delta t^{first}_{display}$ is the time span until the first feedback is presented to the user after a request. This includes the fastest time step's computation time as well as the time span between the time instant this result arrives and the point in time it is shown in the animation. The number of visible gaps $g_{visible}$ in the animation—that is, the number of discrete time steps whose visualization result is not available when the animation reaches this time step—is a measure for the continuity of the time-varying visualization.

A direct comparison of these two visibility measures for ten repeated measurements of the *static* scheduling and the *continuous visualization* scheduling are given in Table 7.1. In each repetition, we varied the moment in visualization time at which the time-varying visualization was requested randomized. These measurements were conducted using eight worker nodes. Input parameters for the *continuous visualization* strategies were the speed-up (without caching) depicted in Figure 7.8—which is used as number of service stations p — and the worst case computation time from Figure 7.4— which is used as deterministic computation time $\bar{t}_{comp}$. Using these parameters, the *continuous visualization* strategy adapted the animation time per time step t_{frame} to 0.12 s, that is, 8.3 time steps were shown per second. We employed the same animation speed during display of the results obtained by the *static* scheduling.

While the *static* scheduling produced between 26-40 gaps during animation, the *continuous visualization* scheduling did not produce any gaps. The high scatter of the number of gaps using the *static* scheduling is explained by the fact that we varied the moment in visualization time at which the time-varying visualization was requested. This resulted in different starting points in the animation for each measurement, while the computational order for the *static* scheduling remained the same. Therefore, each time a different number of gaps occured. The time instant the request is issued also affects the waiting time to the first visible result. Depending on the user's position in visualization time, the time until the first result is visible to the user when using the *static* scheduling varies significantly between 0.63 - 3.97 s, resulting in an average value of 2.39 s. By employing the *continuous visualization* strategy, the first visible time step is predicted and scheduled early, therefore the average waiting time is reduced to 0.3 s.

	static	continuous
$g_{visible}$	26-40	0
avg. $\Delta t^{first}_{display}$	2.39 s	0.3 s

Table 7.1.: Visibility measurements comparing the *static* and *continuous visualization* strategies.

Local Investigation Strategy

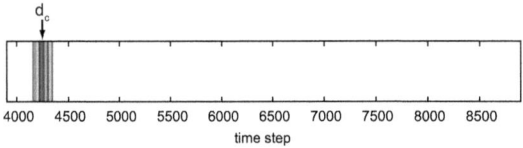

Figure 7.16.: Arrival distribution with *local investigation* scheduling for a small temporal neighborhood of size $m = p$. Darker time steps arrive earlier than brighter ones.

Figure 7.16 shows the result arrival times for a *local investigation* user-centered scheduling. Starting from the paused position d_c, results arrive in the neighborhood whose size m equals the number of available processors p. While the utilized ranking function prioritizes data from left-to-right in the animation direction and right-to-left in the other direction, Figure 7.16 shows that time steps arrive in a different order. This is explained by the small request size. Because each worker node computes a single time step only, the whole neighborhood is concurrently computed. Waiting times in the task queue due to the order of the time steps do not occur. Therefore, the individual computation time of each subtask strongly influences the corresponding result's arrival time. For instance, the leftmost subtask in the neighborhood that has been assigned to highest rank value arrives earlier than results in the animation's direction, because the individual computation time for this time step is faster than that of the other subtasks. Nonetheless, because the visible time step d_c is computed in the first distribution phase of the dynamic scheduling, the waiting time until a first result is visible is significantly reduced. For larger $m > p$, the obtained arrival times show the desired behavior.

7.6. Summary and Discussion

In this chapter, we have presented a parallel system for computation of time-varying visualizations. Based on the Viracocha framework, we have improved both software-technical usage and performance for time-independent visualizations. We have discussed and evaluated several dynamic scheduling strategies, one of which was particularly designed to incorporate Viracocha's data management. In addition to performance-optimizing scheduling strategies, we have introduced user-centered scheduling techniques that support the user's analysis goal.

The application of parallel computing to the computation of time-independent visualizations has shown to be an effective means to deal with time-varying data. Reported previous work has shown, that overall runtimes can be reduced to a different tolerance class of waiting times. In particular, for requests that take tens of seconds on a single processor, an interactive workflow can be maintained using current compute clusters. Nontheless, for large time-varying data a prior reduction of the data, either by subsampling (see Chapter 6) or by focussing on a selected time interval (see Section 4.2), is often inevitable.

While a good scalability can be achieved when computing time-independent visualization in parallel, file I/O and result transmission remain bottlenecks. Viracocha's data management helps to reduce file I/O by caching and prefetching data. Because the visualization application is the single receiver for the concurrently produced result data, a high-performance connection to the worker nodes is desirable to remedy this transmission bottleneck. As an alternative solution, additional transmission channels to transport results concurrently to the visualization system could be employed. Such a scenario is, for instance, useful if the visualization application does not run on a single machine, but is executed on a distributed system itself—e.g., to drive a room-mounted display like a CAVE or PowerWall. Then, result data can be transmitted to each visualization machine and put together into a complete animation on the visualization system, perhaps avoiding the single system bottleneck.

Regarding scheduling techniques, *static* scheduling performed well for balanced tasks, in particular when required data was already cached. However, in realistic scenarios the caches will not contain the entire data set, which leads to inferior performance of *static* scheduling. Here, the *dynamic (g,c)* strategy provides a good comprimise between dynamic balancing and cache efficiency. For unbalanced visualization tasks, *dynamic(1)* scheduling was superior to all other techniques. Though, in general it is hard to decide a-priori if a request will be unbalanced or balanced. For this reason, we consider the guided scheduling techniques as a compromise solution for general tasks whose load balance is not known beforehand.

The user-centered scheduling strategies represent a new characteristic of scheduling strategies that

CHAPTER 7. A PARALLEL SYSTEM FOR TIME-VARYING VISUALIZATIONS

is established by the specific use case of parallel computing within an interactive environment. Instead of targeting high performance, these techniques target a fast achievement of the user's analysis goal. While the shown result arrivals intuitively match to assumed user goals, these scheduling techniques are heuristic approaches. The identification of the user's current goal as well as the assessment of a shown visualization w.r.t. the achievement of this goal are open problems. However, in our opinion, including the user's behavior directly in the computational process is an essential step in order to analyze large time-varying data.

CHAPTER 8

SUMMARY AND CONCLUSION

The goal of this thesis, as defined in Chapter 1, has been to address the *interaction* and *computation problems* that occur when analyzing large time-varying data. We have not proposed new visualization techniques to analyze scientific data. Instead, the techniques we have introduced support the usage of available visualization techniques by providing data structures, temporal travel techniques, reduced temporal samplings, or exploitation of parallel resources. Our goal has not been to replace existing approaches, but to augment them in order to enable an efficient analysis of large time-varying data.

In the scientific visualization community, visualization of large time-varying data, in particular interaction with and the analysis process of such data, is a relatively new topic. Consequently, besides focussing on our primary goals, this thesis fundamentally contributes to this newly emerging topic by introducing several classifications and taxonomies to structure and classify multiple parts of the analysis process.

As a conceptual foundation to describe solutions to both *interaction* and *computation problems*, we have introduced a time model to formalize the term *time* as it occurs in scientific visualization. This model has enabled us to define necessary data structures in order to manage large time-varying data. Modeling operations that allow reuse of data and mixing of heterogeneous simulations have been presented. Interaction operations that provide a formalism to describe user interaction on these data structures have been proposed. To exemplarily show the gained advantages, we have described in detail two complex visualization applications that significantly benefit from the realization of our model. The introduced notation is also applied throughout this thesis, which has enabled a precise description of temporal properties.

CHAPTER 8. SUMMARY AND CONCLUSION

In order to address the *interaction problem*, we first have elaborated a task taxonomy that identifies and classifies user interaction with respect to time in the scientific data analysis process. This taxonomy has enabled us to discuss possible user interfaces that are applicable in a virtual environment. We have shown several exemplary user interfaces that can be employed to navigate in time. In addition, the taxonomy exposed "empty spots" of temporal navigation subtasks, that is, temporal navigation tasks that are typically not covered in scientific visualization toolkits. Based on this task taxonomy we have proposed several novel direct manipulation techniques to solve temporal navigation tasks. This includes, for instance, dragging a virtual object along its trajectory as well as selecting a box-shaped region in order to show all active movements inside this region. In a user study we have conducted, simulation scientists executed certain travel tasks faster and more accurately by directly interacting in the spatial domain of the simulation compared to using a common 2D user interface. In addition, the users' subjective preferences clearly identified this direct manipulation interface as a viable solution for the target user group.

To conclude the *interaction problem*, navigation in large time-varying data is eased by a more intuitive interaction in the spatial domain that does not operate directly on the highly resolved discrete time steps any more. Similarly, the implicit description of what the user assesses important is an intuitive way to select a temporal resolution. In both methods, our approach has been to remove the necessity to operate on the large number of time steps directly and instead of enabling the user to formulate his goal independently of the actual time steps (e.g., by using spatial input, temporal patterns or sketches). Reducing the temporal resolution also contributes to the *interaction problem*, because conventional temporal interaction techniques—e.g. a time slider—are again applicable when the resolution is reduced to a few hundred time steps only.

To reduce the *computational problem*, we have followed a two-step approach. In the first step, the high temporal resolution of large time-varying data is sampled down to a lower resolution. In the second step, visualizations based on the down-sampled resolution are computed using a parallel system, where discrete time steps are processed concurrently. By incorporating user preference and experience in the sampling process, the coarser resolution is non-uniformly adapted to resolve important temporal regions. The users can describe their preferences for certain phenomena by a combination of importance functions. We have shown multiple examples for these functions, which include hand-drawn sketches, information theory, or temporal patterns of simulated attribute data. Depending on the desired target resolution, our sampling algorithm computes within acceptable waiting times a trade-off solution that satisfies multiple importance functions. The evaluation has shown that our approach can achieve the same expressiveness of a time-varying phenomenon—as defined by the importance functions—using significantly less time steps compared to using a common uniform subsampling.

In order to manage this down-sampled temporal resolution, we have described the parallel computation system Viracocha that is connected as a compute backend to a virtual environment. We have shown several improvements to concurrently compute time steps, which included technical aspects as well as algorithmic aspects. The improved Viracocha system efficiently exploits available resources and is able to reduce overall runtimes to a tolerable waiting time. In particular, for requests that take tens of seconds on a single processor, an interactive workflow can be maintained using current compute clusters. Furthermore, multiple scheduling strategies, which distribute independent time steps to processes, have been developed and analyzed. A new class of scheduling strategies has been introduced that takes the interactive usage scenario into consideration. The proposed heuristics reorder compute tasks, such that the arrival of visible result data is arranged in order to achieve certain analysis goals faster. We have shown results that indicate that these user-centered scheduling strategies provide a further benefit for interactive analysis of large time-varying data.

To conclude the *computational problem*, the desired quality of the temporal resolution and the available parallel resources are the key factors that influence the degree of reduction of the *computational problem*. An arbitrarily large number of time steps can be subsampled, but the desired target resolution influences both the subsampling time and the resulting computation time to visualize the data. A scalable system that makes the most of the available computing resources can reduce waiting time significantly. But unless a huge amount of processors is available, a prior focussing on selected time steps using subsampling or a focussing on a temporal interval by the user is still inevitable to reduce the computational load. The user-centered scheduling strategies further contribute to focus the available computational resources to the user's current goal. While faster visualization algorithms are still desirable to deal with large data, our approaches provide at once a benefit for a large class of algorithms—that is, time-independent visualization algorithms.

The described techniques have all been realized in the ViSTA FlowLib visualization software; the time model is even a core component of this software library. The technical embedding into this Virtual Reality framework allows a straightforward use of the developed methods within a variety of virtual environments. This integration facilitates an easy deployment of the developed techniques into other research projects based on the same toolkit.

The introduced foundations open up multiple possibilities and problems that could be topics of future research. Non-uniform approaches to speed selection and resolution selection will be necessary in order to analyze large time-varying data in a reasonable time. While some recent publications addressed these topics (e.g., mutual information based resolution selection [101] or speed selection based on identified trends [112]), in our opinion substantial research in this area is still required. Besides more effective computing and interaction techniques, this includes investigation about perceptional issues and comprehension of time-varying data. The latter topic is

CHAPTER 8. SUMMARY AND CONCLUSION

related to the question of effective wayfinding techniques in the temporal domain, that is, "How can the creation of a mental map for complex time-varying processes be supported?"

Besides these general aspects of interaction with time-varying data, our results have shown that direct interaction approaches provide a major benefit for VR-based scientific visualization setups. We believe that a similar desktop-based 3D user interface could be a major improvement in the analysis of dynamic phenomena. However, the efficient translation from a 3D input used inside an immersive scene to a desktop-setup remains future work. In addition, other alterations than an object's movements could be exploited to navigate in time, for instance, growing movements or alteration of an object's scalar attributes.

Regarding temporal resolution, the objective assessment of a sampling's quality with respect to the visualized phenomena has not been fully solved. In this thesis, we have assessed the quality of a sampling by the distance to an assumed optimum in objective space. Though, this rather technical measure does not reveal if the sampling was sufficient to answer the user's analysis question. Furthermore, while we have discussed the design and evaluation of our subsampling approach with domain scientists, the selection algorithm has not yet been evaluated in daily work. Such an application in real world use cases may give useful hints to the assessment of temporal resolutions and might allow a more detailed analysis of the *select resolution* subtask in temporal navigation. In addition, while the proposed multi-objective optimization algorithms obtained good results, the lack of scalability as well as runtimes of several seconds for larger target resolutions impede the usage of our approach in certain cases. Improving the runtime behavior by parallelizing the proposed algorithms or the application of a different optimization algorithm may avoid this problem. Such algorithms may even be able to subsample future large time-varying data interactively.

A similar statement holds for interaction-based scheduling strategies. While we have shown technical measurements and exemplary arrival behavior of result data, for the assessment of a scheduling's quality with respect to the analysis goal, user studies with domain scientists are inevitable. But, such studies are hard to conduct because they require a well thought-out design, careful selection of test data, and several voluntary domain scientists. Nontheless, methodically observing the analysis behavior of domain scientists when investigating time-varying data will provide convincing evaluation of interaction-related and user-centered techniques and perhaps it will even point out areas of future research.

To summarize, several interesting topics are left open, which create the need for future research. Despite these open topics, in this thesis, we have elaborated and evaluated techniques that provide feasible solutions to the *interaction* and *computational problem* when working with large time-varying data.

APPENDIX A

TERMINOLOGY

A.1. Overview of the Time Model

Continuous time frames	
User time	$U \subset \mathbb{R}^+$
$\downarrow \hat{u}$	$\hat{u}(u) = \frac{u-u_0}{u_1-u_0}$
Visualization time	$V = [0,1] \subset \mathbb{R}$
$\downarrow \hat{v}$	$\hat{v}^{(k)}(v_0^{(k)}) = s_{start}^{(k)}$, $\hat{v}^{(k)}(v_1^{(k)}) = s_{end}^{(k)}$
Simulation time	$S = [s_{start}, s_{end}] \subset \mathbb{R}^+$
$\downarrow \hat{s}$	$\hat{s}(s_{start}) = i_0$, $\hat{s}(s_{end}) = i_{m-1}$
Discrete time frames	
Time indices	$I = (i_0, \ldots, i_{m-1}) : i_j \in \mathbb{N}_0$
$\downarrow \hat{i}$	$\hat{i} : I \to P$
Time steps	$P = \{p_0, \ldots, p_{n-1}\} : p_i \in \mathbb{N}_0$

Table A.1.: Summary of the time frame notation with notation and numeric domain of the five time frames and the corresponding mappings between time frames (denoted with a hat).

As an additional constraint, the mapping $\hat{i}$ has to respect the correlation between a time step p_j and the corresponding simulation time s_j: $\hat{i}(i) = p_j \Rightarrow s_j \in \hat{s}^{-1}(i)$.

In this thesis, we use the following shorthand notation: $\hat{u}^* : U \to P$ is defined by the concatenation of all mappings from user time to time steps: $\hat{u}^*(t) = \hat{i} \circ \hat{s} \circ \hat{v} \circ \hat{u}(t)$. This function $\hat{u}^*$ retrieves to a user time the corresponding time step.

APPENDIX A. TERMINOLOGY

A.2. Terms and Definitions

3D interaction Human-computer interaction in which the user's tasks are performed directly in a 3D spatial context [14].

interaction technique A method allowing a user to accomplish a task via a user interface (UI). An interaction technique includes both hardware (input/output devices) and software components. The interaction technique's software component is responsible for mapping the information from the input device (or devices) into some action within the system, and for mapping the output of the system to a form that can be displayed by the output device (or devices) [14].

Model-View-Controller (MVC) is a design pattern [38], which is often applied to construct user interfaces. This paradigm consists of three objects: model, view, and controller. The model represents the application object, the view its visual representation, and the controller determines the interaction with the model.

position control Interaction that maps user input directly to a position, that is, time instant or time interval for temporal navigation.

rate control Interaction that maps user input to a movement rate, for instance, animation speed or stepsize for discrete movement.

request In Chapter 7, the visualization system sends *requests* for time-varying visualization data to the Viracocha parallel system. A *request* comprises the description and parametrization of a visualization algorithm as well as the description of the algorithm's input data.

subtask In Chapter 7, each *task* is decomposed into a collection of *subtasks* in order to compute the task concurrently. In this thesis, we regard each discrete time step that is processed by a time-independent visualization as a single *subtask*.

task In Chapter 7, a *task* represents a currently processed request from a visualization system. A *task* is computed by a work group, which consists of a group of worker nodes managed by a task controller.

time-dependent visualization algorithm Time-dependent visualization algorithms are algorithms that require multiple time steps in order to work and introduce a dependency between single time steps (see Section 2.1.1).

A.2. TERMS AND DEFINITIONS

time-independent visualization algorithm Time-independent visualization algorithms are algorithms that process multiple time steps independently from each other (see Section 2.1.2).

time-varying data In the context of scientific visualization, in time-varying data at least one data attribute (e.g., scalar, vector or tensor) varies with time at a discrete location. In flow simulation, such a flow is often called unsteady or transient flow. Therefore, in this work, we will use the terms *unsteady* and *transient* synonymous to time-varying.

user-centered scheduling A class of scheduling strategies that uses a ranking function to decide the order of computation for a list of given time steps. Single time steps are prioritized based on the user's current analysis goal with the time-varying visualization. Examples for these strategies are proposed in Section 7.4.2.

user interface (UI) The medium through which the communication between users and computers take place. The UI translates a user's actions and state (inputs) into a representation the computer can understand and act upon, and it translates the computer's actions and state (outputs) into a representation the human user can understand and act upon [56].

visualization In Chapter 7, we use the term *visualization* to denote any kind of visualization primitives or geometric data that are produced during the visualization process and are used as input for the rendering step. In general, visualization is often defined as a method of computing that transforms symbolic information into geometric information [49].

APPENDIX B

IMPLEMENTATION DETAILS

This section contains technical and implementation-specific details concerning the time model (see Section B.1) and further improvements of the Viracocha system for computation of time-varying visualizations (see Section B.2). The details presented here are not necessary to understand the corresponding concepts already described in the appropriate chapters. But, they may ease the usage or re-implementation of several techniques described in this thesis.

B.1. Time Model

The time model described in Chapter 3 is implemented by the ViSTA FlowLib library [87]. Because ViSTA FlowLib targets visualization of time-varying scientific data, the described time model represents a core component of this library. The embedding of the model into the FlowLib software was realized as described in the following section: A central *visualization controller* manages all objects that need to be rendered. Therefore, it maintains the current user time—using the computer's system time—and the current visualization time. Both user and visualization time are independent from any specific simulation data and are therefore managed in this central component. In order to ensure that at each point in visualization time the correct objects for this time value are displayed, each time-varying object is linked to a *time mapper*. A time mapper exists for each distinct simulation k and contains information about the simulation time frame $S^{(k)}$, the time indices $I^{(k)}$, the time steps $P^{(k)}$, and the mapping functions between those. Using this time mapper, the visualization controller can determine for each object—which corresponds to a certain simulation—the correct discrete result data.

APPENDIX B. IMPLEMENTATION DETAILS

The interface of the time mapper is depicted at the end of this section in Figure B.2. The interface contains methods *GetSimulationTime*, *GetTimeIndex*, and *GetTimeStep*, which implement the necessary mapping functions $\hat{s}^{(k)}, \hat{i}^{(k)}, \hat{p}^{(k)}$ for a specific simulation k. To construct the time mapper, an implicit and an explicit mode are supported. The explicit construction is done by specifying the set of n time indices $\{i_0 = (s_{i_0}, d_{i_0}), i_1 = (s_{i_1}, d_{i_1}), \ldots, (s_{i_{n-1}}, d_{i_{n-1}})\}$, where each time index is described by the corresponding time step and the midpoint of the corresponding simulation time interval. The implicit constructor is a convenience method to construct uniform samplings with a fixed time step stride and time steps that possess uniformly distributed simulation time values.

B.2. Improving Performance

As described in Section 7.3.1, we identified three major causes for serial overhead when computing time-independent visualizations using Viracocha: the overhead associated with the creation of a new task, the overhead due to returning result data in the client-server architecture, and the visualization algorithm itself. The former problem has already been discussed in Section 7.3.1. The latter problems require technical solutions that are described in this appendix.

In order to reduce the time required for data transmission, which is necessary to return data to the client, we overlapped this communication with computation [28]. Because we separated the command and data transmission code fragments in the software model, separating the corresponding control flows is straightforward. We implemented this separation by applying a producer-consumer scheme with a single producer thread and a single consumer thread. The DataLaViSTA transmission strategy acts as a data producer, that is, the visualization algorithm produces result data. This data is collected in a shared queue (cf. Section 7.3.2) that synchronizes producer and consumer thread. The data consumer is an active component that sends all data in the shared queue using a TCP/IP connection to the client and sleeps whenever no result data is available. This construction enables an overlapping of the computation task (data producer) and the data transmission task (data consumer).

The optimization of the visualization algorithm itself cannot be realized by the Viracocha system. Viracocha provides only interfaces (e.g., scheduling strategy, data transmission strategy, or interprocess communication) that can be utilized in a visualization algorithm's implementation. Therefore, optimization of this algorithm is the task of the visualization developer. With the growing availability of multicore computers, thread-level parallelization has become an efficient way of optimization. Parallelization standards like OpenMP [11] simplify the development of parallel code. Such a parallelization has to be part of the algorithm's implementation and is therefore not

B.2. IMPROVING PERFORMANCE

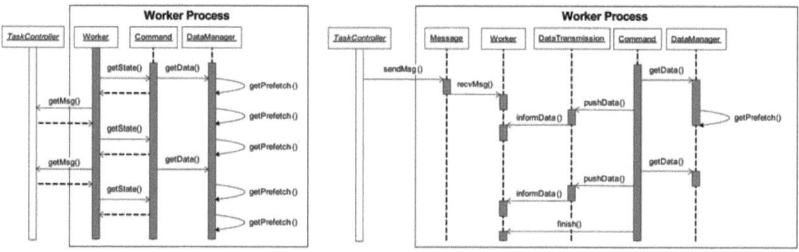

Figure B.1.: UML-like sequence diagram of the worker's control flow. Left: Three threads (worker, command, data manager) operate in busy waiting mode. Right: Two more threads are employed (i.e., messages and data transmission), but all five threads operate in idle waiting mode reducing CPU time.

discussed here. However, Viracocha can support parallel visualization algorithms by provision of thread-safe implementations of offered interfaces as well as by thrifty resource consumption of the Viracocha system.

Because the improved Viracocha itself employs multiple threads to operate, thread-safety has been taken care of. However, Viracocha employed a busy waiting scheme for several threads (see Section 7.2). That is, to check if a condition is fulfilled (i.e., "has a message arrived?" or "is the command finished?") the threads frequently evaluate the condition (also called *spinning*). While this is a fine-grain access control, this spinning wastes processor CPU cycles [32]. An alternative provided by most systems (e.g., POSIX threads) are condition variables that enable a thread to wait for a Boolean predicate. While waiting, the thread does not actively consume processor resources. Figure B.1 shows the situation before (left) and after the changes (right) in an UML-like sequence diagram. In the initial state, three threads were continuously active. To create well-defined condition variables, the worker thread's subtasks of receiving messages and data transmission to the client were extracted into own components. By using condition variables threads are only active when their particular task is required (e.g., receiving a message for the messages thread or managing the worker state for the worker thread). Only the command is continuously active while a task is computed. This deallocation of processor resources enables a possibly higher speed-up for other thread-level parallelizations, as available resource are allocated more thriftily.

In Wolter et al. [110], we used OpenMP to resample tetrahedral grids onto Cartesian grids for efficient particle tracing on a GPU. We showed that this thread-level parallelization scaled well up to 16 OpenMP threads within a Viracocha command. In Hentschel at al. [53, 54], we employed OpenMP to speed-up point selection for brushing multidimensional queries in virtual environments. We reduced the update latency—that is, the time until the first result arrived—with a parallel efficiency of 83% with up to 8 OpenMP threads.

APPENDIX B. IMPLEMENTATION DETAILS

```cpp
class CVveTimeMapper
{
public:

class CImplicitTimings
{
public:
CImplicitTimings();
~CImplicitTimings();

int    m_iNumberOfIndices; /* number of time indices */
int    m_iNumberOfSteps;   /* number of time steps */
int    m_iFirstStep;       /* number of the first time step */
int    m_iStepStride;      /* stride of the time steps */
float  m_fVisStart;        /* start time (in visualization time) */
float  m_fVisEnd;          /* end time (in visualization time) */
float  m_fSimStart;        /* start time (in simulation time) */
float  m_fSimEnd;          /* end time (in simulation time) */
};

CVveTimeMapper(const CImplicitTimings &oImplicitTimings);


/* every time index corresponds to one of these internal structures*/
struct sExplicitIndexInfo
{
int m_iTimeStep; /* this is the number of this time step */
float m_fSimTime; /* the simulation time value for this time step */
};

CVveTimeMapper(const std::vector<sExplicitIndexInfo> &oExplicitTimings);


/**
 * Returns the simulation time for the given visualization time.
 */
 float GetSimulationTime(float fVisTime);

/**
 * Returns the time index for the given simulation time.
 */
 int GetTimeIndex(float fSimTime);

/**
 * Returns the time step for the given time index.
 */
 int GetTimeStep(int iIndex);

};
```

Figure B.2.: C++ interface of the time mapper class.

APPENDIX C

DATA SETS

C.1. Nasal Airflow

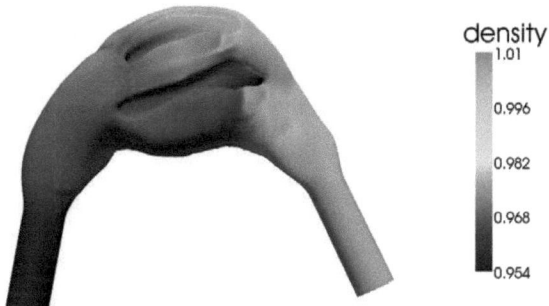

Figure C.1.: Geometry of the nasal cavity, colored by (dimensionless) density.

The human nasal cavity has to satisfy a variety of different functions. Besides respiration it is responsible for moistening, tempering, and cleaning the air. Impaired nasal respiration, in particular under normal breathing conditions, i.e., in everyday life situations, is a common and widespread disease, which makes nose surgery one of the most often performed operations in the world. The main goal of the interdisciplinary project underlying this work is to gain better insights into the complex flow inside the human nasal cavity.

The simulation of the unsteady flow of nasal respiration (see Figure C.1) is courtesy of the Institute of Aerodynamics (AIA) at RWTH Aachen University. The simulation for this flow field was

APPENDIX C. DATA SETS

performed on a multi-block grid, which was later converted into a tetrahedral grid. The data set resolves a full respiration cycle, i.e., one inhalation and exhalation period, with a high temporal resolution. For the analysis, the 2nd out of 4 such cycles with a small overlap to the first and third cycle was chosen, resulting in 5000 discrete time steps and 132 GB of raw data. Characteristics of the data set are listed in Table C.1.

Nasal airflow statistics	
vertices per time step	279,181
cells per time step	262,784
size on disk per time step	27.07 MB
time steps	5000
total size on disk	132.15 GB

Table C.1.: Statistics of the nasal airflow data set.

C.2. Geothermal Reservoir Simulation

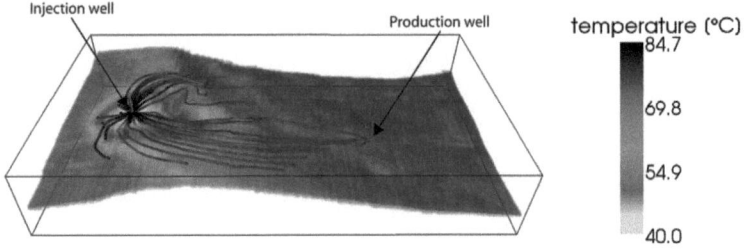

Figure C.2.: Visualization of the geothermal data set. The contour shows a surface of similar rock characteristics and is colored by temperature. The shown pathlines show the movement of injected water. Hot water is produced, used for heating, and then reinjected at lower temperatures. After several tens of years, this injected water reaches the producer, heated by geothermal energy. Thus the production of warm water is maintained.

In this geothermal reservoir simulation, a planned deep geothermal installation with one hot water production well and one cold water injection well is projected (see Figure C.2). Fluid flow and heat transport through porous rocks during the operation of the installation are simulated. The study presented here focuses on the prediction of reservoir temperatures and production behavior which is crucial for planning a deep geothermal installation. The forecasting horizon is 100 years with a nearly weekly time resolution, resulting in 5000 discrete time steps and approximately 55 GB of raw data. This regular grid data is courtesy of Geophysica Beratungsgesellschaft mbH and the Institute of Applied Geophysics and Geothermal Energy. Details are listed in Table C.2.

Geothermal simulation statistics	
vertices per time step	170,560
cells per time step	161,280
size on disk per time step	11.06 MB
time steps	5000
total size on disk	54.01 GB

Table C.2.: Statistics of the geothermal data set.

C.3. Ventricular Assist Device

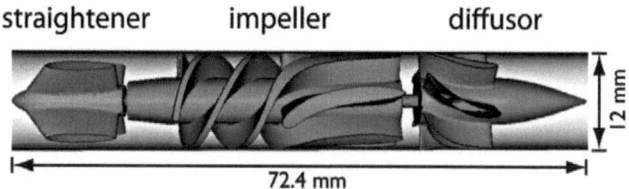

Figure C.3.: Geometry of the DeBakey blood pump. Blood flows from left to right through the straightener, the rotating impeller, and the diffusor geometries. The device is implanted to assist the left ventricle.

This use case is the visualization of the MicroMed DeBakey VAD® (Ventricular Assist Device). This data set was provided by the Chair for Computational Analysis of Technical Systems (CATS). Ventricular assists devices help to bridge the waiting time until a suitable heart transplant is available. The goal of this project is to analyze the hematologic effect of hemolysis—that is, the release of hemoglobin of red blood cells due to elevated stress—that can occur within an artifical blood pump.

The device consists of three components: the *straightener*, the *diffusor*, and the *impeller*, as shown in Figure C.3. These components are integrated into a cylindrical casing, which is not shown in the figure. The pump is used to transport blood at desired flow rates between 2 and 5 l/min. For the simulation described in this section the impeller was set to a constant rate of rotation of 7500 rpm, yielding a flow rate of 2 l/min. All other parts of the geometry remain static.

Empirical measurements show a mean velocity of about 0.4414 m/s which results in a mean residence time of 0.288 s. Consequently, a portion of blood will be transported from start to end in average in 36 full rotations. The used visualization shows 10,000 discrete time steps for 50 rotations of the rotating impeller. The rotation itself is cyclic, i.e., 200 discrete time steps are sufficient to depict a single rotation. However, along the full 10,000 time steps, 2,000 particle traces to evaluate the rate of hemolysis were computed, resulting in 1 GB of raw data.

Details on the visualization of blood damage inside this simulated VAD can be found in Hentschel

APPENDIX C. DATA SETS

et. al. [52]. Data set characteristics are listed in Table C.3.

Ventricular assist device statistics	
vertices per time step	630,693
cells per time step	3,714,611
size on disk per time step	135.54 MB
time steps	200
total size on disk	26.47 GB

Table C.3.: Statistics of the Ventricular Assist Device data set.

C.4. Metal Forming Process Chain

This material science simulation does not consist of a single data set, but multiple data sets generated by different simulation tools. Each tool simulates a different aspect of the processed material. The tools are organized in a virtual process chain that exchanges information about the entire material and its history between the various simulation tools. Goal of this project is to simulate the final material properties after heterogeneous processing steps. This data set describes the complete simulation of a gear wheel construction [105] and is courtesy of the Cluster of Excellence "Integrative Production Technology for High-Wage Countries".

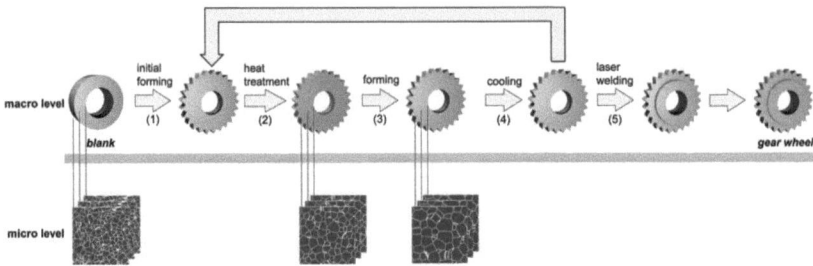

Figure C.4.: Overview of the virtual process chain to simulate the generation of a gear wheel. Starting with a steel-alloy blank and after an initial forming process (1), the workpiece is iteratively heated (2), formed (3) and cooled down (4) again. Finally, a ring component is laser welded (5) to the work piece. The result is a completed gear wheel.

The virtual process chain comprises five processing steps that are depicted in Figure C.4. Starting with an alloyed steel blank, an initial forming step (1) creates a gear wheel shape. In the next three processing steps (2-4), this gear wheel is heated, formed, and cooled again. Steps 2 and 3 are simulated both on a macroscopic level (overall characteristics of the entire wheel) and a microscopic level (microstructure simulation of a small region within the wheel). The heating, forming and cooling steps are repeated several times to improve material properties (a so called

C.4. METAL FORMING PROCESS CHAIN

annealing process). Finally, in a last step (5), a ring component is laser welded to the processed gear wheel.

The metal forming process chain that describes the forming of a gear wheel consists of a set of seven individual data sets. Each data set was simulated by a different simulation tool. The result is not only a mixture of data sets with heterogeneous temporal characteristics, but also multiple geometrical characteristics.

First, we list the five data sets that are used to simulate the process on the macroscopic scale. The data set describing the first phase—i.e., the initial forming—represents only $\frac{1}{8}$ of the gear's geometry due to spatial symmetry. The whole gear wheel can be generated by rotation of this segment. The simulation data is currently under development, therefore only small data sets and a low temporal resolution were available (see Table C.4). The forming, heat treatment and cooling phases utilize the same geometry and temporal resolution, which is described in Table C.5. The used unstructured hexahedral geometry represents the entire gear wheel because symmetry does not hold for all three phases. While the different process steps utilize the same spatial and temporal resolution, they differ in the simulated scalar attributes. The last step in the macroscopic simulation is the laser welding phase. This data set comprises tetrahedral elements and a high temporal resolution. The statistics of the laser welding data set are listed in Table C.6.

In the microscopic simulation, both phases—i.e., forming and heat treatment—share the same spatial and temporal structure like in the macroscopic simulation. However, the microscopic data set has a finer spatial and temporal resolution. The identical statistics of the two microscopic data sets are listed in Table C.7.

Initial forming	
vertices per time step	875
cells per time step	615
size on disk per time step	0.19 MB
time steps	21
total size on disk	4 MB

Table C.4.: Statistics of the (macroscopic) initial forming data set.

APPENDIX C. DATA SETS

Forming, heat treatment and cooling, macro scale	
vertices per time step	59,608
cells per time step	56,430
size on disk per time step	15 MB
time steps	19
total size on disk	285 MB

Table C.5.: Statistics of the (macroscopic) forming data set. Heating and cooling simulations use the same data structure.

Laser welding	
vertices per time step	256,684
cells per time step	1,370,285
size on disk per time step	69.6 MB
time steps	360
total size on disk	24.5 GB

Table C.6.: Statistics of the (macroscopic) laser welding data set.

Forming and heat treatment micro scale	
vertices per time step	23,328,000
cells per time step	23,069,699
size on disk per time step	180 MB
time steps	52
total size on disk	9.1 GB

Table C.7.: Statistics of the micro-scale forming data set. Microscopic heat treatment utilizes the same data structure.

BIBLIOGRAPHY

[1] Christopher Ahlberg and Ben Shneiderman. The Alphaslider: a Compact and Rapid Selector. In *Proceedings of the SIGCHI Conference on Human Factors in Computing Systems*, pages 365–371, 1994.

[2] James Ahrens, Kristi Brislawn, Ken Martin, Berk Geveci, C. Charles Law, and Michael Papka. Large-Scale Data Visualization using Parallel Data Streaming. *IEEE Computer Graphics and Applications*, 21(4):34–41, 2001.

[3] Wolfgang Aigner, Alessio Bertone, Silvia Miksch, Christian Tominski, and Heidrun Schumann. Towards a Conceptual Framework for Visual Analytics of Time and Time-Oriented Data. In *Proceedings of the 2007 Winter Simulation Conference*, pages 721–729, 2007.

[4] Wolfgang Aigner, Silvia Miksch, Wolfgang Müller, Heidrun Schumann, and Christian Tominski. Visualizing Time-Oriented Data: A Systematic View. *Computers & Graphics*, 31(3):401–409, 2007.

[5] Hiroshi Akiba and Kwan-Liu Ma. A Tri-Space Visualization Interface for Analyzing Time-Varying Multivariate Volume Data. In *Proceedings of Eurographics/IEEE VGTC Symposium on Visualization*, pages 115–122, 2007.

[6] Hippocrates G. Apostle. *Aristotle's Physics*. Indiana University Press, 1969. Translated with Commentaries and Glossary.

[7] Ingo Assenmacher. *Low Latency Technology for Interactive Virtual Environments*. PhD thesis, RWTH Aachen University, 2008.

Bibliography

[8] Ingo Assenmacher, Bernd Hentschel, Marc Wolter, and Torsten Kuhlen. DataLaVista: A Packet-based Pipes and Filters Architecture for Data Handling in Virtual Environments. In *3. Workshop der GI-Fachgruppe VR/AR, Koblenz*, pages 25–36, 2006.

[9] Gordon V. Bancroft, Fergus J. Merritt, Todd C. Plessel, Paul G. Kelaita, R. Kevin Kelaita, and Al Globus. FAST: A Multi-Processed Environment for Visualization of Computational Fluid Dynamics. In *Proceedings of IEEE Visualization '90*, pages 14–27, 1990.

[10] John Biddiscombe, Berk Geveci, Ken Martin, Kenneth Moreland, and David Thompson. Time Dependent Processing in a Parallel Pipeline Architecture. *IEEE Transactions on Visualization and Computer Graphics*, 13(6):1376–1383, 2007.

[11] OpenMP Architecture Reviewer Board. OpenMP Application Program Interface, v2.5, 2005.

[12] Doug A. Bowman and Larry F. Hodges. Formalizing the Design, Evaluation, and Application of Interaction Techniques for Immersive Virtual Enviroments. *Journal of Visual Languages and Computing*, 10:37–53, 1999.

[13] Doug A. Bowman, David Koller, and Larry F. Hodges. Travel in Immersive Virtual Environments: An Evaluation of Viewpoint Motion Control Techniques. In *Proceedings of the IEEE Virtual Reality Annual International Symposium (VRAIS)*, pages 45–52, 1997.

[14] Doug A. Bowman, Ernst Kruijff, Joseph J. LaViola, and Ivan Poupyrev. *3D User Interfaces: Theory and Practice*. Addison-Wesley Professional, 2004.

[15] Ralph Bruckschen, Falko Kuester, Bernd Hamann, and Kenneth I. Joy. Real-Time Out-of-Core Visualization of Particle Traces. In *Proceedings of the IEEE Symposium on Parallel and Large-Data Visualization and Graphics*, pages 45–50, 2001.

[16] Steve Bryson. Time, Data-Time, and Real-Time Interactive Visualization. *Computational Physics*, 11(3):270–274, 1997.

[17] Steve Bryson and Michael Gerald-Yamasaki. The Distributed Virtual Windtunnel. In *Proceedings of Supercomputing '92*, pages 275–284, 1992.

[18] Steve Bryson and Sandy Johan. Time Management, Simultaneity and Time-Critical Computation in Interactive Unsteady Visualization Environments. In *Proceedings of IEEE Visualization '96*, pages 255–261, 1996.

[19] Kai Bürger, Polina Kondratieva, Jens Krüger, and Rüdiger Westermann. Importance-Driven Par-

ticle Techniques for Flow Visualization. In *Proceedings of IEEE VGTC Pacific Visualization Symposium*, pages 71–78, 2008.

[20] Florian Cajori. *Sir Isaac Newton's Mathematical Principles of Natural Philosophy and his System of the World*. University of California Press, 1962.

[21] Steven P. Callahan, Juliana Freire, Juliana Freire, Emanuele Santos, Carlos E. Scheidegger, Claudio T. Silva, and Huy T. Vo. Managing the Evolution of Dataflows with VisTrails. In *Proceedings of the 22nd International Conference on Data Engineering Workshops*, page 71, 2006.

[22] Stephen M. Casner. Task-analytic Approach to the Automated Design of Graphic Presentations. *ACM Transactions on Graphics*, 10(2):111–151, 1991.

[23] Li Chen, Issei Fujishiro, and Kengo Nakajima. Optimizing Parallel Performance of Unstructured Volume Rendering for the Earth Simulator. *Parallel Computing*, 29(3):355–371, 2003.

[24] Min Chen, David Ebert, Hans Hagen, Robert S. Laramee, Robert van Liere, Kwan-Liu Ma, William Ribarsky, Gerik Scheuermann, and Deborah Silver. Data, Information, and Knowledge in Visualization. *IEEE Computer Graphics and Applications*, 29(1):12–19, 2009.

[25] Computational Engineering International Inc. EnSight 8.2. Information available online at www.ensight.com (last visited 2009/12/11).

[26] Robert B. Cooper. *Introduction to Queuing Theory*. Elsevier North Holland, Inc., second edition, 1981.

[27] Thomas M. Cover and Joy A. Thomas. *Elements of Information Theory*. Wiley, Hoboken, New Jersey, second edition, 2006.

[28] David E. Culler and Jaswinder Pal Singh. *Parallel Computer Architecture - A Hardware/Software Approach*. Morgan Kaufmann Publishers, 1999.

[29] Indraneel Das and John Dennis. A Closer Look at Drawbacks of Minimizing Weighted Sums of Objectives for Pareto Set Generation in Multicriteria Optimization Problems. *Structural Optimization*, 14(1):63–69, 1997.

[30] Gerwin de Haan, Michal Koutek, and Frits H. Post. IntenSelect: Using Dynamic Object Rating for Assisting 3D Object Selection. In Erik Kjems and Roland Blach, editors, *Proceedings of the 9th International Immersive Projection Technology Workshop (IPT) and 11th Eurographics Workshop on Virtual Environment (EGVE)*, pages 201–209, 2005.

Bibliography

[31] Kalyanmoy Deb. *Multi-Objective Optimization using Evolutionary Algorithms*. Wiley-Interscience Series in Systems and Optimization. John Wiley & Sons, Chichester, 2001.

[32] Jack Dongarra, Ian Foster, Geoffrey Fox, William Gropp, Ken Kennedy, Linda Torczon, and Andy White. *Sourcebook of Parallel Computing*. Morgan Kaufmann Publishers, 2003.

[33] Pierre Dragicevic, Gonzalo Ramos, Jacobo Bibliowitcz, Derek Nowrouzezahrai, Ravin Balakrishnan, and Karan Singh. Video Browsing by Direct Manipulation. In *Proceedings of the SIGCHI Conference on Human Factors in Computing Systems*, pages 237–246, 2008.

[34] Robert M. Edsall, Menno-Jan Kraak, Alan M. MacEachren, and Donna J. Peuquet. Assessing the Effectiveness of Temporal Legends in Environmental Visualization. In *Proceedings of GIS/LIS '97*, pages 677–685, 1997.

[35] David Ellsworth, Bryan Green, and Patrick Moran. Interactive Terascale Particle Visualization. In *Proceedings of IEEE Visualization 2004*, pages 353–360, 2004.

[36] Niklas Elmqvist and Philippas Tsigas. A Taxonomy of 3D Occlusion Management for Visualization. *IEEE Transactions on Visualization and Computer Graphics*, 14(5):1095–1109, 2008.

[37] Steven Feiner and Dore D. Seligmann. Cutaways and Ghosting: Satisfying Visibility Constraints in Dynamic 3D Illustrations. *The Visual Computer*, 8(5-6):292–302, 1992.

[38] Erich Gamma, Richard Helm, Ralph Johnson, and John Vlissides. *Design Patterns: Elements of Reusable Object-Oriented Software*. Addison Wesley, 1995.

[39] Andreas Gerndt. *Methoden des parallelen Postprocessing numerischer Strömungssimulationsdaten für die echtzeitfähige Visualisierung und Interaktion in VR-basierten Arbeitsumgebungen*. PhD thesis, RWTH Aachen University, 2006.

[40] Andreas Gerndt, Bernd Hentschel, Marc Wolter, Torsten Kuhlen, and Christian Bischof. Viracocha: An Efficient Parallelization Framework for Large-Scale CFD Post-Processing in Virtual Environments. In *Proceedings of the 2004 ACM/IEEE Conference on Supercomputing*, 2004. Published on CD-ROM.

[41] Andreas Gerndt, Stefan Lankes, Mark Asbach, Thomas Bemmerl, Torsten Kuhlen, and Christian Bischof. Conceptual Design and Implementation of a Pipeline-Based VR-System Parallelized by CORBA, and Comparison with Existing Approaches. In *International Conference on Virtual Reality Continuum and its Applications in Industry*, pages 368–374, 2004.

[42] Andreas Gerndt, Samuel Sarholz, Marc Wolter, Dieter an Mey, Christian Bischof, and Torsten

Kuhlen. Particles and Continuum—Nested OpenMP for Efficient Computation of 3D Critical Points in Multi-Block CFD Datasets. In *Proceedings of the 2006 ACM/IEEE Conference on Supercomputing*, 2006. Published on CD-ROM.

[43] Andreas Girgensohn, John Boreczky, and Lynn Wilcox. Keyframe-Based User Interfaces for Digital Video. *Computer*, 34(9):61–67, 2001.

[44] Markus Glatter, Jian Huang, Sean Ahern, Jamison Daniel, and Aidong Lu. Visualizing Temporal Patterns in Large Multivariate Data using Textual Pattern Matching. *IEEE Transactions on Visualization and Computer Graphics*, 14(6):1467–1474, 2008.

[45] John Goldman and Trina M. Roy. The Cosmic Worm. *IEEE Computer Graphics and Applications*, 14(4):12–14, 1994.

[46] Eric J. Griffith, Michal Koutek, Frits H. Post, Thijs Heus, and Harm J. J. Jonker. A Reprocessing Tool for Quantitative Data Analysis in a Virtual Environment. In *Proceedings of the ACM Symposium on Virtual Reality Software and Technology (VRST)*, pages 212–215, 2006.

[47] Robert Haimes. pv3: A Distributed System for Large-Scale Unsteady CFD Visualization. Technical Report AIAA 94-0321, American Institute of Aeronautics and Astronautics, 1994.

[48] Robert Haimes and Dave Darmofal. Visualization in Computational Fluid Dynamics: a Case Study. In *Proceedings of IEEE Visualization '91*, pages 392–397, 1991.

[49] Charles D. Hansen and Chris R. Johnson, editors. *The Visualization Handbook*. Elsevier Academic Press, 2004.

[50] Mark Harrower, Amy L. Griffin, and Alan MacEachren. Temporal Focusing and Temporal Brushing: Assessing their Impact in Geographic Visualization. In *Proceedings of the 19th International Cartographic Conference*, pages 14–21, 1999.

[51] Bernd Hentschel. *Interactive Feature Analysis in Virtual Environments*. PhD thesis, RWTH Aachen University, 2009.

[52] Bernd Hentschel, Irene Tedjo, Markus Probst, Marc Wolter, Marek Behr, Christian Bischof, and Torsten Kuhlen. Interactive Blood Damage Analysis for Ventricular Assist Devices. *IEEE Transactions on Visualization and Computer Graphics*, 14(6):1515–1522, 2008.

[53] Bernd Hentschel, Marc Wolter, and Torsten Kuhlen. Virtual Reality-Based Multi-View Visualization of Time-Dependent Simulation Data. In *IEEE Virtual Reality Conference Poster Proceedings*, pages 253–254, 2009.

[54] Bernd Hentschel, Marc Wolter, Peter Renze, Wolfgang Schröder, Christian Bischof, and Torsten Kuhlen. Hybrid Parallelization for Multi-View Visualization of Time-Dependent Simulation Datasets. In *Proceedings of the Eurographics Workshop on Parallel Graphics and Visualization (EGPGV'09)*, pages 79–86, 2009.

[55] Ken Hinckley, Edward Cutrell, Steve Bathiche, and Tim Muss. Quantitative Analysis of Scrolling Techniques. In *Proceedings of the SIGCHI Conference on Human Factors in Computing Systems*, pages 65–72, 2002.

[56] Deborah Hix and Rex H. Hartson. *Developing User Interfaces: Ensuring Usability Through Product & Process (Wiley Professional Computing)*. Wiley, 1993.

[57] Ingolf Hörschler, Wolfgang Schröder, and Matthias Meinke. Comparison of Steady and Unsteady Nasal Cavity Flow Solutions for the Complete Respiration Cycle. *Computational Fluid Dynamics Journal*, 15(3):354–377, 2006.

[58] Wolfgang Hürst, Georg Gotz, and Tobias Lauer. New Methods for Visual Information Seeking Through Video Browsing. In *Proceedings of the IEEE International Conference on Information Visualisation (IV '04)*, pages 450–455, 2004.

[59] Wolfgang Hürst and Patrick Stiegeler. User Interfaces for Browsing and Navigation of Continuous Multimedia Data. In *Proceedings of the 2nd Nordic Conference on Human-Computer Interaction (NordiCHI '02)*, pages 267–270, 2002.

[60] Heike Jänicke, Alexander Wiebel, Gerik Scheuermann, and Wolfgang Kollmann. Multifield Visualization Using Local Statistical Complexity. *IEEE Transactions on Visualization and Computer Graphics*, 13(6):1384–1391, 2007.

[61] Vijendra Jaswal. CAVEvis: Distributed Real-Time Visualization of Time-Varying Scalar and Vector Fields using the CAVE Virtual Reality Theater. In *Proceedings of IEEE Visualization '97*, pages 301–308, 1997.

[62] Jinhee Jeong and Fazle Hussain. On The Identification of a Vortex. *Journal of Fluid Mechanics*, 285:69–94, 1995.

[63] Alark Joshi and Penny Rheingans. Illustration-Inspired Techniques for Visualizing Time-Varying Data. *Proceedings of IEEE Visualization '05*, pages 679–686, 2005.

[64] Thorsten Karrer, Malte Weiss, Eric Lee, and Jan Borchers. DRAGON: A Direct Manipulation Interface for Frame-Accurate In-Scene Video Navigation. In *Proceedings of the SIGCHI Conference on Human Factors in Computing Systems*, pages 247–250, 2008.

BIBLIOGRAPHY

[65] Don Kimber, Tony Dunnigan, Andreas Girgensohn, Frank Shipman, Tao Turner, and Tao Yang. Trailblazing: Video Playback Control by Direct Object Manipulation. In *Proceedings of the IEEE International Conference on Multimedia and Expo*, pages 1015–1018, 2007.

[66] Scott Kirkpatrick, C. D. Gelatt Jr., and Mario P. Vecchi. Optimization by Simulated Annealing. *Science*, 220:671–680, 1983.

[67] Kitware, Sandia National Labs, and CSimSoft. ParaView 3.0 - Parallel Visualization Application. Available online at www.paraview.org (last visited 2009/12/11).

[68] Yuichi Koike, Atsushi Sugiura, and Yoshiyuki Koseki. TimeSlider: An Interface to Specify Time Point. In *UIST '97: Proceedings of the 10th Annual ACM Symposium on User Interface Software and Technology*, pages 43–44, 1997.

[69] Oliver Kreylos, Tony Bernardin, Magali I. Billen, Eric S. Cowgill, Ryan D. Gold, Bernd Hamann, Margarete Jadamec, Louise Kellogg, Oliver G. Staadt, and Dawn Y. Sumner. Enabling Scientic Workflows in Virtual Reality. In *Proceedings of of the ACM SIGGRAPH International Conference on Virtual Reality Continuum and Its Applications (VRCIA 2006)*, pages 155–162, 2006.

[70] Eric Lee, Henning Kiel, and Jan Borchers. Scrolling Through Time: Improving Interfaces for Searching and Navigating Continuous Audio Timelines. Technical Report AIB-2006-17, RWTH Aachen University, Department of Computer Science, 2006.

[71] Orna Lichtenstein, Amir Pnueli, and Lenore D. Zuck. The Glory of the Past. In *Proceedings of the Conference on Logic of Programs*, pages 196–218. Springer-Verlag, 1985.

[72] Aidong Lu and Han-Wei Shen. Interactive Storyboard for Overall Time-Varying Data Visualization. In *Proceedings of IEEE Pacific Visualization Symposium*, pages 143–150, 2008.

[73] Kwan-Liu Ma. Visualizing Time-Varying Volume Data. *Computing in Science & Engineering*, 5(2):34–42, 2003.

[74] Kwan-Liu Ma and Steven Parker. Massively Parallel Software Rendering for Visualizing Large-Scale Data Sets. *Computer Graphics and Applications*, 21(4):72–83, 2001.

[75] Stéphane Marchesin, Catherine Mongenet, and Jean-Michel Dischler. Dynamic Load Balancing for Parallel Volume Rendering. In *Proceedings of Eurographics Symposium on Parallel Graphics and Visualization (EGPGV '06)*, pages 43–50, 2006.

[76] Robert B. Miller. Response Time in Man-Computer Conversational Transactions. In *AFIPS Conference Proceedings*, pages 267–277, 1968.

BIBLIOGRAPHY

[77] Mark Monmonier. Strategies for the Visualization of Geographic Time-Series Data. *Cartographica*, 27(1):30–45, 1990.

[78] Constantine D. Polychronopoulos and David J. Kuck. Guided Self-Scheduling: A Practical Scheduling Scheme for Parallel Supercomputers. *IEEE Transactions on Computers*, C-36(12):1425–1439, 1987.

[79] Frits H. Post, Benjamin Vrolijk, Helwig Hauser, Robert S. Laramee, and Helmut Doleisch. The State of the Art in Flow Visualisation: Feature Extraction and Tracking. *Computer Graphics Forum*, 22(4):775–792, 2003.

[80] Prabhat, Andrew Forsberg, Michael Katzourin, Kristi Wharton, and Mel Slater. A Comparative Study of Desktop, Fishtank, and Cave Systems for the Exploration of Volume Rendered Confocal Data Sets. *IEEE Transactions on Visualization and Computer Graphics*, 14(3):551–563, 2008.

[81] Zenon W. Pylyshyn. *Seeing and Visualizing: It's Not What You Think (Life and Mind)*. Bradford Books, 2003.

[82] Freek Reinders, Frits H. Post, and Hans J.W. Spoelder. Visualization of Time-Dependent Data with Feature Tracking and Event Detection. *The Visual Computer*, 17(1):55–71, 2001.

[83] Philip K. Robertson. A Methodology for Scientific Data Visualisation: Choosing Representations based on a Natural Scene Paradigm. In *Proceedings of IEEE Visualization '91*, pages 114–123, 1990.

[84] Trina M. Roy, Carolina Cruz-Neira, and Thomas A. Defanti. Cosmic Worm In The Cave: Steering A High Performance Computing Application From A Virtual Environment. *Presence: Teleoperators and Virtual Environments*, 2(4):121–129, 1995.

[85] Gerik Scheuermann and Xavier Tricoche. Topological Methods for Flow Visualization. In Chris R. Johnson and Charles D. Hansen, editors, *Visualization Handbook*, chapter 14, pages 341–356. Elsevier Academic Press, 2004.

[86] Marc Schirski, Christian Bischof, and Torsten Kuhlen. Employing Graphics Hardware for an Interactive Exploration of the Airflow in the Human Nasal Cavity. In *Proceedings of Medicine Meets Virtual Reality*, pages 409–411, 2007.

[87] Marc Schirski, Andreas Gerndt, Thomas van Reimersdahl, Torsten Kuhlen, Philipp Adomeit, Oliver Lang, Stefan Pischinger, and Christian Bischof. ViSTA FlowLib - A Framework for Interactive Visualization and Exploration of Unsteady Flows in Virtual Environments. In *Proceedings of the 7th*

International Immersive Projection Technology Workshop (IPT) and 9th Eurographics Workshop on Virtual Environment (EGVE), pages 77–85, 2003.

[88] Marc Schirski, Torsten Kuhlen, Martin Hopp, Philipp Adomeit, Stefan Pischinger, and Christian Bischof. Virtual Tubelets - Efficiently Visualizing Large Amounts of Particle Trajectories. *Computers & Graphics*, 29(1):17–27, 2005.

[89] William Schroeder, Ken Martin, and Will Lorensen. *The Visualization Toolkit - An Object-Oriented Approach to 3D Graphics*. Kitware, Inc., 4 edition, 2006.

[90] Heidrun Schumann and Wolfgang Müller. *Visualisierung - Grundlagen und allgemeine Methoden*. Springer, 2000.

[91] Han-Wei Shen. Isosurface Extraction in Time-Varying Fields using a Temporal Hierarchical Index Tree. In *Proceedings of IEEE Visualization '98*, pages 159–166, 1998.

[92] Han-Wei Shen, Ling-Jen Chiang, and Kwan-Liu Ma. A Fast Volume Rendering Algorithm for Time-Varying Fields using a Time-Space Partitioning (TSP) Tree. In *Proceedings of IEEE Visualization '99*, pages 371–377, 1999.

[93] Kevin I. Smith, Richard M. Everson, Jonathan E. Fieldsend, Chris Murphy, and Rashmi Misra. Dominance-Based Multiobjective Simulated Annealing. *IEEE Transactions on Evolutionary Computation*, 12(3):323–342, June 2008.

[94] Jason S. Sobel, Andrew S. Forsberg, David H. Laidlaw, Robert C. Zeleznik, Daniel F. Keefe, Igor Pivkin, George E. Karniadakis, Peter Richardson, and Sharon Swartz. Particle Flurries - Synoptic 3D Pulsatile Flow Visualization. *IEEE Computer Graphics and Applications*, 24(2):76–85, 2004.

[95] Rebecca R. Springmeyer, Meera M. Blattner, and Nelson L. Max. A Characterization of the Scientific Data Analysis Process. In *Proceedings of IEEE Visualization '92*, pages 235–242, 1992.

[96] Philip Sutton and Charles D. Hansen. Isosurface Extraction in Time-Varying Fields using a Temporal Branch-on-Need Tree (T-BON). In *Proceedings of IEEE Visualization '99*, pages 147–153, 1999.

[97] Colin Swindells, Melanie Tory, and Rebecca Dreezer. Comparing Parameter Manipulation with Mouse, Pen, and Slider User Interfaces. *Computer Graphics Forum*, 28(3):919–926, 2009.

[98] Irene Tedjo-Palczynski, Bernd Hentschel, Marc Wolter, Thomas Beer, and Torsten Kuhlen. Toolkit-Independent Interaction Specification for VR-based Visualization. In *Proceedings of ACM Symposium on Virtual Reality Software and Technology (VRST)*, pages 263–264, 2009.

[99] Andries van Dam, Andrew Forsberg, David H. Laidlaw, Joseph LaViola, and Rosemary Michelle Simpson. Immersive Virtual Reality for Scientific Visualization: A Progress Report. *IEEE Computer Graphics and Applications*, 20(6):26–52, 2000.

[100] Ivan Viola, Armin Kanitsar, and Meister Eduard Gröller. Importance-Driven Volume Rendering. In *Proceedings of IEEE Visualization '04*, pages 139–145, 2004.

[101] Chaoli Wang, Hongfeng Yu, and Kwan-Liu Ma. Importance-Driven Time-Varying Data Visualization. *IEEE Transactions on Visualization and Computer Graphics*, 14(6):1547–1554, 2008.

[102] Stephen Wehrend and Clayton Lewis. A Problem-Oriented Classification of Visualization Techniques. In *Proceedings of IEEE Visualization '90*, pages 139–143, 1990.

[103] Daniel Weiskopf and Gordon Erlebacher. Overview of Flow Visualization. In Charles D. Hansen and Christopher R. Johnson, editors, *The Visualization Handbook*, pages 261–278. Elsevier Academic Press, 2004.

[104] Marc Wolter, Ingo Assenmacher, Bernd Hentschel, Marc Schirski, and Torsten Kuhlen. A Time Model for Time-Varying Visualization. *Computer Graphics Forum*, 28(6):1561–1571, 2009.

[105] Marc Wolter, Thomas Beer, Philippe Cerfontaine, Bernd Hentschel, and Torsten Kuhlen. Interactive Simulation Data Exploration in Virtual Environments. In *Proceedings of the 2nd Sino-German Workshop "Virtual Reality & Augmented Reality in Industry"*. Springer, 2009. in print.

[106] Marc Wolter, Christian Bischof, and Torsten Kuhlen. Dynamic Regions of Interest for Interactive Flow Exploration. In *Proceedings of the Eurographics Symposium on Parallel Graphics and Visualization (EGPGV '07)*, pages 53–60, 2007.

[107] Marc Wolter, Andreas Gernd, Torsten Kuhlen, and Christian Bischof. Markov Prefetching in Multi-Block Particle Tracing. In *Parallel Computational Fluid Dynamics 2006*, pages 27–34. Elsevier, 2007.

[108] Marc Wolter, Bernd Hentschel, Marc Schirski, Andreas Gerndt, and Torsten Kuhlen. Time Step Prioritising in Parallel Feature Extraction on Unsteady Simulation Data. In *Proceedings of the Eurographics Symposium on Parallel Graphics and Visualization (EGPGV '06)*, pages 91–98, 2006.

[109] Marc Wolter, Bernd Hentschel, Irene Tedjo-Palczynski, and Torsten Kuhlen. A Direct Manipulation Interface for Time Navigation in Scientific Visualizations. In *Proceedings of the IEEE Symposium on 3D User Interfaces*, pages 11–18, 2009.

[110] Marc Wolter, Marc Schirski, and Torsten Kuhlen. Hybrid Parallelization for Interactive Exploration

in Virtual Environments. In *Parallel Computing: Architectures, Algorithms and Applications*, volume 15 of *Advances in Parallel Computing*, pages 79–86. IOS Press, 2007.

[111] Marc Wolter, Irene Tedjo-Palczynski, Bernd Hentschel, and Torsten Kuhlen. Spatial Input for Temporal Navigation in Scientific Visualizations. *IEEE Computer Graphics and Applications*, 29(6):24–34, 2009.

[112] Jonathan Woodring and Han-Wei Shen. Multiscale Time Activity Data Exploration via Temporal Clustering Visualization Spreadsheet. *IEEE Transactions on Visualization and Computer Graphics*, 15(1):123–137, 2009.

[113] Hamid Younesy, Torsten Möller, and Hamish Carr. Visualization of Time-Varying Volumetric Data using Differential Time-Histogram Table. In *Eurographics Workshop on Volume Graphics 2005 (VG'05)*, pages 21–29, 2005.

[114] Hongfeng Yu, Kwan-Liu Ma, and Joel Welling. A Parallel Visualization Pipeline for Terascale Earthquake Simulations. In *Proceedings of the 2004 ACM/IEEE conference on Supercomputing (SC '04)*, 2004. published on CD-ROM.

[115] Robert Zeleznik, Joseph LaViola, Daniel Acevedo, and Daniel Keefe. Pop Through Buttons for Virtual Environment Navigation and Interaction. In *Proceedings of IEEE Virtual Reality*, pages 127–134, 2002.

[116] Shumin Zhai, Barton A. Smith, and Ted Selker. Improving Browsing Performance: A Study of Four Input Devices for Scrolling and Pointing Tasks. In *Proceedings of the IFIP TC13 International Conference on Human-Computer Interaction (INTERACT '97)*, pages 286–293, 1997.

[117] Eckart Zitzler, Marco Laumanns, and Lothar Thiele. SPEA2: Improving the Strength Pareto Evolutionary Algorithm. Technical Report TIK-Report No. 103, Swiss Federal Institute of Technology, 2001.

[118] Mosche Zukerman. Introduction to Queueing Theory and Stochastic Teletraffic Models. Information available online at www.ee.unimelb.edu.au/staff/mzu/classnotes.pdf (last visited 2009/12/11), 2008. Class Notes.

Die VDM Verlagsservicegesellschaft sucht für wissenschaftliche Verlage abgeschlossene und herausragende

Dissertationen, Habilitationen, Diplomarbeiten, Master Theses, Magisterarbeiten usw.

für die kostenlose Publikation als Fachbuch.

Sie verfügen über eine Arbeit, die hohen inhaltlichen und formalen Ansprüchen genügt, und haben Interesse an einer honorarvergüteten Publikation?

Dann senden Sie bitte erste Informationen über sich und Ihre Arbeit per Email an *info@vdm-vsg.de*.

Sie erhalten kurzfristig unser Feedback!

VDM Verlagsservicegesellschaft mbH
Dudweiler Landstr. 99   Telefon +49 681 3720 174
D - 66123 Saarbrücken   Fax   +49 681 3720 1749
www.vdm-vsg.de

Die VDM Verlagsservicegesellschaft mbH vertritt

Printed by Books on Demand GmbH, Norderstedt / Germany